ADVANCE PRAISE

"Franchisees have a better chance of success, as Christy explains, when they have leadership traits, a sound financial footing, commitment and loyalty to the franchise relationship and all the hard and soft skills that go along with these.

'Show up and stay engaged' is a great mantra for franchisees. I agree you can't fix what you haven't measured, so I applaud the focus throughout the book on incorporating metrics-based planning.

The risks Christy took and her unrelenting focus on developing her franchise and then exiting it according to her plans, hold valuable lessons for all entrepreneurs."

Mark Siebert
CEO
The iFranchise Group Franchise Consultants

"If you are a franchisee or planning to become a franchisee Christy Wilson Delk's book is one you've got to read. Even if your franchisor is great at training, Christy is better because she trains from her experiences as a successful franchisee. Read this book!"

Dr. John P. Hayes
Best-selling author: "101 Questions to
Ask Before You Invest in a Franchise"
Titus Chair for Franchise Leadership
Palm Beach Atlantic University

"While the description of our meeting in the Preface may be a bit exaggerated (height - 6'3" at the most), her depiction of the determination and focus that was exhibited in moving forward with her new endeavor was on-the-mark. She accomplished a massive undertaking with limited resources and an abundance of research and planning, bringing the risk level down even for this conservative accountant. When I think of Christy, I think of a person that exemplifies the pursuit of the American Dream. I am happy to be a small part of her business accomplishment from both the start-up phase to ultimate sale… it truly defines entrepreneurial spirit."

Al Ruggiero, CPA
Winter Park, FL

"Christy Wilson Delk will always be considered a part of the Kids 'R' Kids Family. She owned and operated one of our franchises in Florida for many years. Not only did Christy shine in her ownership, she proved to be an asset to our company as a whole. Her book, *Adventures in Franchise Ownership*, is not only spot on with how to grow, protect and focus your business, Christy adds personal experiences, along with a bit of humor, to keep the reader engaged throughout the book. I highly recommend Christy's book if you plan on owning or already own a franchise, in order to become a stronger and more successful franchisee."

Darlene Vinson Barnwell

Kids 'R' Kids Learning Academies –
Chief Creative Officer and daughter
of founder Pat and Janice Vinson

Adventures in Franchise Ownership

Adventures in
FRANCHISE OWNERSHIP

4 Pillars to Strengthen, Protect, and Grow Your Business

Christy Wilson Delk

NEW YORK

LONDON • NASHVILLE • MELBOURNE • VANCOUVER

Adventures in Franchise Ownership

4 Pillars to Strengthen, Protect and Grow Your Business

Published in New York, New York, by Morgan James Publishing. Morgan James is a trademark of Morgan James, LLC. www.MorganJamesPublishing.com

The Morgan James Speakers Group can bring authors to your live event. For more information or to book an event visit The Morgan James Speakers Group at www.TheMorganJamesSpeakersGroup.com.

ISBN 9781683508830 paperback
ISBN 9781683508847 eBook
Library of Congress Control Number: 2017918564

Cover Design by:
Megan Whitney
megan@creativeninjadesigns.com

Interior Design by:
Chris Treccani
www.3dogcreative.net

In an effort to support local communities, raise awareness and funds, Morgan James Publishing donates a percentage of all book sales for the life of each book to Habitat for Humanity Peninsula and Greater Williamsburg.

Get involved today! Visit
www.MorganJamesBuilds.com

This book is dedicated to

Roland Delk
It wouldn't have been an adventure without you

and

Mom
Who supported me from the start

and

My kindred spirits—people who act on their desire to own a business
and the franchisors who make that possible

ACKNOWLEDGMENTS

Strategy and success aside, we know it is relationships that bring true meaning to our adventures in business as in life. Telling Pat and Janice Vinson I was leaving the Kids 'R' Kids Academy family was the hardest part of my decision. (*Theirs* is a story worth telling.) I thank them for the opportunity of a lifetime and thank their children, David Vinson and Darlene Vinson Barnwell, for their devotion and commitment to the "family" business. I also thank the clients (parents *and* especially the children) and the residents of East Orlando for allowing Kids 'R' Kids to be a part of your life and your community. None of this would have been possible without the loving and professional caregivers, teachers, and managers whose dedication made magic happen every day. It was truly an honor and a privilege to serve you and work with you all.

I am indebted to dear friends old and new for supporting me through the adventures and the challenges. I'm especially grateful to Barbara Lanning, Mary "Mimo" Collins, Jerri Johnson, Elissa Eunice, and Joe North, who know me all too well. And my appreciation runs deep for my new friends, the franchisors and franchisees who graciously gave up their time in support of this project, answering my questions and sharing their stories, *some without knowing me at all*. It's the industry's spirit and core value of helping others succeed upon which I drew for motivation while writing this book.

Thankfully, I also had Wendy Kurtz, publishing consultant and agent extraordinaire, to draw upon. Wendy and I had served on a board together years ago. We re-connected at a conference and I quickly realized if anyone would be willing and able to help me, it would be her. Wendy's agency, Elizabeth Charles & Associates, LLC, took me from a basic outline, a few scattered articles, journal entries and Post-It notes to the finished book you are holding in your hands. Along the way, she connected me with Juli Baldwin of The Baldwin Group, who helped organize and craft the tools and techniques I used into what became the 4 Pillars Approach detailed in this book. I also thank Juli for keeping this first-time author focused on the most important person, *you*, the reader.

When Juli had enough, it was Diane Sears of DiVerse Media LLC who took the manuscript and my voice and created a much-needed reader-friendly format. Thank you to my "A-Team" for your shared expertise, consistent encouragement, and sincere desire to see this project to completion. *Four blondes do make it write.* It wouldn't have happened without you.

I would also like to thank freelance editor, Kerry Maffeo, for batting cleanup on the final manuscript and finally, David Hancock at Morgan James Publishing for believing in my vision and helping to get this book out of my computer and into your hands.

And last but certainly not least, I thank you, the reader, for your trust in me when you made the commitment to read this book. I applaud your dedication for investing the time to expand your perspective and focus on what you want *and* deserve to achieve. When it's all said and done, business ownership is an individual sport. So, when you count your friends and fans in the bleachers, be sure to count me among them.

Please write to me when you have something to share. I'd love to hear from you.

It's your turn now.

CONTENTS

PREFACE
This Is How It Started

This is what it had come down to.

It was 1996. I was sitting across the desk from Al Ruggiero. Al is a conservative, mild-mannered accountant and has been my CPA since the mid-1980s.

There he was. All 6-foot-4 of him, standing up *not looking very mild at all*. Things had definitely taken a turn for the dramatic, and Al was visibly upset. He was making arm gestures and noises inferring he was flushing an invisible toilet in response to what I had just told him … that I was about to cash out my 401(k) plan—all $165,000 of it—as a partial down payment to secure a $1.67 million U.S. Small Business Administration loan to purchase a childcare franchise.

Al's enactment was to emphasize taking this money out meant I would be facing a hefty early withdrawal penalty. He said, and I quote: "Christy, you can*not* be serious. You will *literally* be flushing f-o-r-t-y t-h-o-u-s-a-n-d dollars down the toilet." That was the penalty and extra taxes for withdrawing early.

I could certainly understand his concern. Earlier, I had told him I was selling my house in order to use the equity for the franchise fee. He didn't like that either.

Finally, Al sat down, his shoulders slumping a bit. "*Please*, just think about it. That's your retirement fund." I pushed my professionally bound business plan across his desk and said in a soothing tone, "Al, *this* is my retirement now. I'll make the money back." Then he suggested an alternative: "Can't you get a partner … or find an investor … or *something* else?"

I distinctly remember my response, and how good it felt to say it. "No, Al, I want to do this on my own. It's all right here," I said, nodding to the navy-blue plan with the gold-embossed, trademarked hot-air balloon logo printed on the cover. "I can do this."

He thought for a long moment and then sat back in his chair, arms behind his head. "Alright then," he said with a slight smile, saying without words he knew I had made up my mind.

Laying It All on the Line

Breaking this news to Al was a huge step. Until that point, my dream had been a secret. Even though I projected self-assurance during our meeting, I was scared.

I was not in a good place in my personal life. My husband and I were headed for divorce. My son had just turned a year old and was starting to show some developmental delays and I was pretty sure my job was on the line. It wouldn't be the first or even the second time I had been laid off or terminated.

Focusing intensely on my secret was exactly what I had needed. Getting up at 4 a.m. every day to plug away on the business plan before getting ready for work had been a wonderful diversion. Doing fieldwork on my lunch breaks and weekends with my son in tow had kept me hopeful. Hopeful constructing a building, owning and operating a franchise that served a growing community's young families, would allow me to have the career and financial stability I desperately sought. I wanted to be successful, and no matter how hard I worked or how much education I got, I just couldn't seem to find another way.

The stark truth was, I simply could not afford to fail. *Everything* I had was on the line. This was *it*—my best and only shot at real financial success—and I was taking it. There was simply no turning back.

At 35 years of age, I made a decision that changed my life: the decision to open my own business by buying a franchise. In 2012, I made another big decision. It was time to sell. After 15 years of ownership, I sold my franchise for $6 million.

Peaks and Valleys

This book is about what happened and what I learned during those 15 years of franchise ownership. How I managed my business and not only survived, but thrived through three hurricanes, two expansions, one divorce, multiple managers, and too many employees to remember them all.

When I bought my franchise, there were many days when I wondered, "What if this doesn't work?" When I discovered a thief in my ranks, I fantasized about selling and doing something else. *Anything* else. Usually, the tough days were due to cash flow not being what I had counted on or a key employee giving insufficient notice, like when I had to learn how to drive the bus over a weekend.

Every franchisee experiences valleys. Sometimes the weeks and months that follow the opening of a hot new competitor or the agonizing reality of a down economic cycle feel unending. These are the times when the little voice inside your head whispers, "What if this fails?" or "What if *I* fail?" You may wake up nights panic-stricken what you're doing isn't sufficient to push your business back into black, or you can't fall asleep because you're worried about how you will make the next payroll. At times, it feels as if you have no control. I know many of you can relate to these moments of self-doubt.

But there are also those other days. The extra-good days when the pride of ownership and the income and lifestyle it affords lead to feelings of joy, confidence, and thoughts of, "Why would anyone *not* want to own and operate their own franchise?" Hopefully, you have had your fair share of those good times when everything is in blissful balance and you write yourself a substantial check because the bank account is looking good and, after all, you *earned* it. Those exhilarating peaks can often sustain our drive and motivation for prolonged periods.

As a Kids 'R' Kids Academy owner-operator, I experienced all of that. The market downturns (check!), another new competitor opening up around the corner (check!) and periods when I found it difficult to enjoy any of my personal passions and even my relationships. At times, it was pretty scary. I wouldn't admit it then but freely share now.

It wasn't until I sold my franchise and had time to reflect that I gained some clarity about what I had been through, what had been accomplished, and what I had learned. I contemplated which hardships could have been avoided and what *specifically I did that was different* than what most owners do.

The essence of what I learned, practiced and now want to share with you is this: By focusing your energy and resources on four specific, vitally important aspects of your franchise, you can strengthen, protect, and grow your business every year. I call these the 4 Pillars of Successful Franchise Ownership. The pillars are: Layers of Loyalty, Strategic Leadership, and Money Metrics. The fourth pillar, Method Management, provides a systematic and orderly process for building and balancing the other three pillars.

When you concentrate your energy and resources on these four areas in a precise, methodical, and disciplined way, you will be able to run your business more efficiently and more profitably than you could ever have imagined … and enjoy your time doing it. The 4 Pillars Approach was the secret to my successful franchise ownership and exit, and I'm certain it will work for you, too. In fact, I'm betting on it!

Why Read This Book

We are betting people, right? After all, we bet on our franchisor and the business model when we signed the agreement, didn't we? I know I did. If you went all in, then you are counting on this bet to be good. *Really* good. Yet, industry surveys show the average franchise ownership tenure is only seven to eight years.

Perhaps that timeframe is not as surprising to you as it was to me. Admittedly, staying engaged and in control of your business year after year is not easy. Some days I swear I needed a Survival Guide. While this book may not give you all the answers you're seeking, it does tell you what you can and really must do in order to beat that average. More important, it tells you how to achieve long-term professional satisfaction, personal enjoyment, and financial success as a franchise owner. I know, because this book is about exactly what I did—and if I can do it,

I know you can, too. By following my lead and building the 4 Pillars into your franchise, you will:

- Gain more control over your business.
- Retain or regain the initial excitement of ownership.
- Lose the anxiety and thoughts of "What if this doesn't work?" or "Is this all there is?"
- Stay professionally challenged and engaged in your business.
- Get and keep quality employees and loyal clients.
- Enjoy the security and reap the financial and personal rewards of owning a thriving business.

You have already made one very sound decision; to buy a franchise. Franchise ownership is the fastest, best path to successful business ownership. It opens the door for those who want to go into business for themselves but don't have an idea for a product or service they can create or the wherewithal to see it through. I include myself in this category, and it's no coincidence most of us were drawn to franchising for those very reasons. However, the opportunity that pulls us into franchising also creates challenges.

Any given franchise system has a wide range of owners, some with significant experience in business but little to no experience in their new chosen field. That was me. I had business experience but zero time spent in the early childhood industry. Conversely, many franchisees may be a good fit for a particular segment or even a specific brand but have no hands-on business experience or education in that field.

That's precisely why I wrote this book: to inspire and help you, (and your franchisor) by leveling the playing field for all owners regardless of your business background, level of experience, or education. I believe those who will most benefit from reading this book are franchisees who have owned their business for one to seven years and want to beat the average, and those who are looking for *more*. This is the "more." This is the book that will show you how to get to the next tier in your franchise system and then to the next one after that until you are recognized as a leader and a passionate Top Performing Franchisee.

Whether you are an experienced owner or are new to franchising, using the 4 Pillars Approach will set you apart. Before long, your franchisor representative will want to know what you're doing that's different so he or she can share it with others in your system. Make plans now to attend your next owners conference because you'll most assuredly be asked to sit on a special panel to share your success strategies alongside other top performers.

If you have the will to think differently about your business, the desire to learn a new approach, and the drive to follow through with action, this is the book for you. If you commit to the 4 Pillars Approach, I'm betting very soon you will worry less about what you're not doing and instead focus on exactly what you need and want to be doing in order to enjoy owning your franchise with a bank account that makes you proud.

The Question You Are Thinking

Before we get started, I need to answer the question you are probably asking by now. After all, I don't want any distractions to come between you and your reading. Here's the elephant in the room: "Christy, if you were so dang successful, why did you sell?"

I'll start by sharing I unequivocally loved everything about franchise ownership. Even during the really hard times, I enjoyed the challenge. It was, without a doubt, the best thing I've ever done, and I staunchly believe franchising is the best path to successful business ownership for many people in this country and in many other countries throughout the world.

My answer is this: As the years went by, I realized I am one of those people who loves change and challenges. I don't even like going to the same travel destination more than once (except New Smyrna Beach, near my home) and I expanded my franchise twice just for the challenge even though things were going really well. Here's the full transparency: I get bored. Quickly. Thus, after 15 years, I was ready for a full lifestyle change. A big one.

Here's the backstory: When my son turned 18, I was really ready to do something different. The exit was planned well in advance. My Employee of The Year plaque had fifteen spaces. That was intentional. Three plus fifteen equals eighteen years old and off to college, or at least out of the house for Roland Delk and time for something new for me. That something new is teaching business courses at Rollins College in Winter Park, Florida, and working with other franchise owners, like you, who are looking for something more from their business.

My biggest hope now is this book shares my experience in a meaningful, enjoyable way and that it will help you achieve the level of success you want and deserve. It's all in here: the peaks, the valleys, and the days in between. With your professional and financial success as my goal, I humbly offer you stories, examples, and advice from myself and others in the industry who are among the Top Performers in their system, representing over a dozen segments.

If you stick with it, work through the exercises, and apply what is useful for you, then like me and others you'll read about in this book, you'll have the energy, drive, and motivation to be the best franchisee you can possibly be and profit handsomely while doing so.

Now, let's get to work!

INTRODUCTION

What's Missing in Your Business?

or the first few years, like you, I was on a steep learning curve. Learning the industry, the franchise operation, the brand, and the ins and outs of basic business ownership was pretty tough and extremely stressful. Finding and keeping good people, making sure I was going to meet payroll during the slow months, and getting a few good hours of sleep were my only priorities. Relationships were short-changed and family time became buckling the kiddo in the car in order to do the errands on the weekends because I had no time or I was too exhausted to do them during the week.

This scenario is not altogether unexpected for years one through three of a new business, but definitely not what I wanted for the long term. I was doing what my franchisor said to do and putting in the time, so why wasn't it getting any easier? Or better? I was searching for inspiration—something that would help me strengthen, protect, and grow my business so I could have the life *and* the income I had imagined when I bought my franchise.

The question I kept asking myself was, "What's missing?"

The Epiphany

By the end of year four, I had already experienced two challenging *valleys*: the 2002 dot.com economic bubble burst and the 2001 post-9/11 recession. From a business perspective, none of these events were totally brutal in my market segment, but they were certainly no cakewalks. I realized during those times, to a large extent, these were things I could not control. That got me thinking about what I *could* control.

It was during that period I came across the book *Peaks and Valleys* by Spencer Johnson, M.D. I read it voraciously. The general concept of the book is that in order to be successful long term, the wise business owner will learn to adapt the business in a way that smooths out the peaks and valleys of economic cycles and, with the right planning, can continue to grow during market downturns. I wanted to be that wise owner. I decided then I would learn how to strengthen, protect, and grow my business the very best way I could. As the leader of your business, like me, focusing on these aspects of your business must become your number one priority.

The analogy Dr. Johnson put forth, of smoothing out the peaks and valleys, stayed with me and so, too, did a few lingering questions. If I can't control the macro economy, what can I control? Can I impact the local economy enough to sustain revenue growth each year? How can I attract and retain good staff, without busting the bank, so the next employment contraction doesn't affect my service or profitability? What should I systematically focus on each year so there is a higher order to my business, thereby smoothing out the intense highs and difficult lows?

This new knowledge and what I had already experienced is what led me to start thinking and acting differently. I would stay aligned with franchisor processes and programs and, in addition, internally focus my business on four areas going forward. Those four areas gradually became the foundational pillars that guided and drove my business for my remaining tenure. The 4 Pillars Approach didn't come to me in a vision—I had to dig deep. I also read a lot of business books, took notes, and tried things out in "real time." I focused on the areas of my franchise that weren't laid out in the owner's manual and that I knew would make a difference. I now believe the 4 Pillars are the key underpinnings of any truly successful business.

With full transparency, I admit that at the time I wasn't sure I was on the right track. Until I was tested, I couldn't be certain. I would soon find out. I was about to get my first real competitor.

The Test

A competing childcare franchise had just planted a giant "Coming Soon!" sign in an empty field right down the street and people were talking about it. By people, I mean my staff and my clients. *My* people! Even my son pointed to it from his car seat when we drove to and from work each day. There was no getting around it. This was serious. And it was personal. At least to me.

The founders of this competitor were former Kids 'R' Kids franchisees. This was their second location and first franchised unit. They knew exactly what to do and how to do it—and worse, they knew exactly what I knew and how I operated.

Or so they thought. This was my test. Game *on*. This was my business to lose, and I was determined to do everything in my power not to. For the next several months I implemented my new strategy using the 4 Pillars Approach as my guidepost. I focused on methodically building the loyalty, leadership, and metrics I hoped would shore up and protect my business.

As far as my clients were concerned, it was business as usual. I smiled and greeted families in the same way I had done for the past three years. I enlisted my franchisor's help and made sure our customers knew we were part of a larger, stronger franchise system that had value they would not be able to find "elsewhere."

I increased internal communication and made sure my managers and staff were in lockstep with me. Together, we focused intently on the 4 Pillars and it was not *business as usual*. It was better. We all felt it. We were re-invigorated, we were motivated, and the team was performing at a very high level. The change was palpable.

When the competitor opened, there was barely a dip in our business. Sure, I lost a couple of families and a couple of teachers, but there was certainly no valley.

Only good things happened from the changes that were implemented, including a plan and announcement for *our* expansion before the competitor even opened. In a very short amount of time, the new strategic focus and corresponding changes showed me the time was right to grow and that the business, and I, could handle it.

Now I knew beyond a shadow of a doubt that as long as I stayed in entrenched with my franchisor and strategically built the 4 Pillars, I would be able to not only strengthen and protect my business, but also sustain revenue growth for the foreseeable future regardless of what challenges might lie ahead. Better still, the security, lifestyle, and income I had hoped for were within my grasp. *Let's roll!*

Perhaps I should be embarrassed it took a threatening new competitor to provide the momentum I needed to be the best I could be. Instead, I'm grateful because that's when I started developing a better, much more intentional way to run the business. I found what was missing in my business, and with trial and error, practice, and determination, I steadily grew my franchise each year for the next 12 years.

The 4 Pillars Approach

I like thinking about the 4 Pillars this way: When you signed on to be a franchisee, you bought the plans and basic structure for a proven, successful enterprise. You may have been given actual construction blueprints (this is what your building or buildout should look like) and an operations manual (this is how you run it) with detailed daily, weekly, and monthly processes. This is very close to how it happens, right? I know it was for me.

Now that your franchise is established, in order to ensure your continued success and maintain your passion as an owner, it's time to fortify what you have built so that when competitors come, down cycles occur, and the unexpected happens, your business is strong, it's protected, and it continues to grow. After all, this is your dream business and you should expect to enjoy a certain level of success. The 4 Pillars Approach provides the insurance you need to cover your bet by strengthening, protecting and growing your business in a methodical and streamlined way.

Let's look at each of the 4 Pillars. While I have listed them in the order you see here, no one pillar is more important than the other. They work in tandem to create synergies and unexpected benefits to your business.

1. **Layers of Loyalty: Strengthen Your Business**

   Building Layers of Loyalty is the pillar that adds long-term stability to a high-performing franchise. All stakeholders contribute to the long-term sustainable growth and success of your franchise, including employees, clients, the local community, and your franchisor. Loyalty ensures market forces and competitors don't have a lasting impact on your profitability and extends your reach and goodwill with negligible costs. It's never too soon or too late to strengthen your business strategically by layering loyalty internally and externally. I would not have been able to expand my business twice if it weren't for the good relationships and loyalty I had built with my franchisor and the others who mattered most. These relationships are a significant component of your success and make being a franchisee all the more enjoyable.

2. **Strategic Leadership: Protect Your Business**

   Leading strategically is a fresh take on leadership, aligning practical leadership processes and methods with your time constraints and your vision for your franchise on an annual basis. Of the many roles and responsibilities you have as a franchise owner, it's mission-critical you lead strategically and shape your success in order to have the business you envision. Leading your business strategically protects your franchise and fortifies it each year, in part, because you have customized it to fit your values and goals and local market. I was one person, with 50 employees, 500 families to serve, and a child to raise. Being strategic about how I invested my leadership time and energy was imperative to my success *and my sanity*. I'm confident it will work for you, too.

3. **Money Metrics: Grow Your Business**

   Knowing your money metrics is foundational for building and growing your franchise. More than the basic details of your company finances, money metrics include franchisor data, industry norms, and your own performance history to compare and then project into the future. In its basic form, understanding your metrics means you are able to know and project with reasonable certainty how an increase in one expense will add or detract from your bottom line, and therefore how much money you will make in a given year. For me, there was simply no substitute for incorporating metrics-based planning and performance measurements for achieving annual profit and revenue goals. Developing and maintaining a true competitive advantage are also part of this foundational pillar.

4. **Method Management: Focus Your Business**

Method management puts success outcomes directly within your control because it is the "how-to" part of building the pillars. Starting with an annual review and organizational accountability, Method Management gives you the framework and timeline to Build Loyalty and Lead Strategically using your Money Metrics as a baseline. Frankly, it's the least-sexy part of how franchisees become successful (which is why I saved it for the end of the book). But it is perhaps the most important pillar, because without it, you most likely will not be able to build the other three pillars long-term. Annual planning, programs, and accountability are not riveting subject matter, but they are the cement that holds your business together.

By methodically and simultaneously building your pillars—layer by layer and year after year—your success, and the income you make, will be solely determined by you. Instead of valleys, the lows will become small dips that will be expected and managed and the highs will become rolling hills that lift you to the next level or point you to expansion or a second unit. You will find, over time, the 4 Pillars are cross-functional. For example, while Money Metrics is the primary pillar to focus on to grow your business, it also helps you strengthen and protect it.

Enjoy Your Business Again

You may think transitioning to the 4 Pillars Approach will be complicated and difficult. In fact, it's the opposite. With Method Management, this approach is implemented systematically. Many of the suggestions create synergies that have a positive impact and build upon other aspects of your business that are already in place.

You may also think that by focusing on the 4 Pillars, you will have less time and fewer resources to devote to franchisor programs, your family, and your personal pursuits. You will not. Building loyalty, leading strategically, and using money metrics to guide your decisions and actions results in increased freedom and flexibility, not less. In fact, you will gain time and energy, allowing more opportunity to focus on the things you enjoy most about your business and your life.

So, what *is* the risk of following my advice and building the 4 Pillars? That's a fair question. A little background and then my take on it.

For the last two years, I've been teaching a course called *Business Innovation and Entrepreneurial Thinking* at Rollins College in Winter Park, Florida. It's a fascinating class and serves as Business 101 for this highly regarded and well-heeled small liberal arts college. (I didn't design the course and so take zero credit for the content.) Besides working with the students, the best part about teaching is that I learn something new every day. In one of the units, we discuss the upside of taking risks: specifically, how not trying something new, such as opening a new business (or implementing the 4 Pillars Approach) comes at a price. For you, the price is that you deny yourself the experience of learning something more in-depth about yourself and your business, developing new relationships, and most important, taking advantage of the synergies and surprises that come from thinking about your business in a different way.

My challenge to you? Commit to yourself to move to the next level in your franchise system; or better still, get into the top tier of your franchise system by implementing the 4 Pillars Approach. You have nothing to lose and everything to gain. Get out of the 80 percent and be in the top 20 percent.

Eighty percent of business owners do little if anything to systematically strengthen, protect, and grow their businesses. They choose not to act. Not because they don't care, but because they don't know specifically what to do. Like you, I've read enough books and heard enough experts tell me what I should do. I'd leave thinking, "Well, that certainly makes sense," only to realize I didn't have a clue as to what to do next, or even where to start. That's not the case with the 4 Pillars. (It's all here.) That leads me to my next and final challenge: Read the book in its entirety. By the end, you'll be more confident and very comfortable using the ideas and tools to strengthen, protect, and grow your franchise *and your future*.

Throughout each of the four sections, I'll share many ways you can systematically and easily incorporate Loyalty, Leadership, Money Metrics, and Method Management into your daily business. Each chapter starts with a quote from a Top Performing Franchisee that I met, mostly by phone, after contacting their home office. These folks are among the most successful people found in franchising and I am so grateful and humbled they took the time to review the chapter-specific questions and provide their most thoughtful answers. Their insights, motivation and willingness to contribute to this project reassured me that not only is franchising good for people, but in our industry, good people abound.

Within the chapters, I'll provide examples of how I used the 4 Pillars Approach. I want you to know what worked and sometimes, what didn't work. I'll tell you the good, the bad, and the really tough aspects of my experience. Full transparency starts now. I will lay bare my professional life and even some of my personal life because, as you well know, when you're a business owner the two are intertwined.

Ready to get started? You already have a great structure. Your franchisor handed you the plans and showed you what to do when you handed him or her the check. Now it's up to you to make sure your structure reflects your values and leadership, and that it fits your personal, professional, and financial definition of success.

Let's begin by strengthening your franchise and Building Layers of Loyalty, the first pillar.

LAYERS OF LOYALTY

Strengthen Your Business

I slept very well at night during the economic recession of 2008 and with more than a dozen new competitors opening in my local market because of the strategies and programs we had in place to address loyalty. I built it, they came. I expanded it, twice, and they still came. Building loyalty into all areas of your franchise is a vital component for long-term franchise success because it reinforces your business and stabilizes your structure, allowing it to withstand the challenges that will inevitably come your way.

If you need convincing, consider what loyalty can do.

It's your *loyal* clients who keep your cash flowing while you work on bringing in the new ones to grow your revenue. It's *loyalty* that helps you attract and retain good employees, keeping your expenses down and your level of service high. It's community *loyalty* you earn over time through your good acts and local engagement that protects your business through downturns and many other challenges that strike every franchise owner sooner or later.

Having a loyalty plan that touches every area of your business helps ensure you are building relationships with people who care about you and the health of your business. That's why it is a foundational pillar and why I devoted an entire section to "intentionally and purposefully" building Layers of Loyalty. We'll use strategies and programs that target your clients, your employees, and your community.

If you already have programs in place, we'll add on. Or you can start fresh and develop brand new ones. The goal is to keep your clients, your staff, and your community invested in your business because when they are invested, they refer and attract others to your business. If you have a plan in place and it's not accomplishing this goal, it may be time to retire it and try something completely fresh.

Franchisor loyalty is the final component of loyalty I strongly encourage you to build. Being a loyal franchisee pays big dividends. I'm living proof of that. I seriously doubt I would be writing this book with a bank account that afforded me this opportunity if I did not have an excellent relationship with Pat and Janice Vinson, my franchisors. I also suspect, between you and me, franchisors are the easiest target out of the four to approach for meaningful success. The vast majority crave good relationships with loyal franchisees and quickly respond and recognize those who make the effort.

But before we talk about building loyalty, you first need to identify your "Sweet Spots." Your business depends on these most valuable clients, employees, and community partners.

CHAPTER 1

Identify Your Sweet Spots

We consider this a relationship-building business. Early on we thought, "Oh my gosh, we can't work this hard!" That's when we intentionally decided to focus our culture on our reputation and all of the people involved. To us, that means building trust. Sometimes we hired and invested in team members before we could even really afford to, but it strengthened our reputation and trust with clients, and that brings word-of-mouth referrals. We also work hard to maintain strong trust bonds with caseworkers, discharge planners, and others who can help us grow our business. We know the magic is in the model!

Jeff Tews and Susan Rather

Madison, Wisconsin
BrightStar Care franchisees since 2006
Multi-unit owners who consistently rank
among the very top of the BrightStar Care system

"Do you know who 'Sweet Spot' customers are?"

That's the question I often open with when I present to franchisees. Some people immediately nod their head. Most folks, though, sort of look around the room, unsure of their answer.

Then I follow up with, "How about your Sweet Spot employees?" That usually gets a few murmurs and mumbles.

"Sweet Spot community partners?" I can usually be assured of blank stares at that point.

Your Sweet Spots are your *ideal* clients, employees, and community partners. They are the very best of the best, the kind of people you wish all your clients, employees, and partners were. If you're going to build a base of rabidly loyal clients, employees, and partners, it seems the place to start would be with knowing who you actually want to attract and keep.

Jeff Tews and Susan Rather clearly know. Throughout the interview, Jeff articulated how they build lasting relationships through trust and focus intently on referral sources that can help them grow their business. Focusing on these types of constituents helps you to strengthen your business by smoothing out the peaks and valleys and synergistically decreases much of the stress inherent in so many workplaces.

Sweet Spot Client

This is your very best client, in profiled form. It's a family that frequently tells others to dine in your restaurant. It's a real estate company that continues to add to its holdings and thereby increases its weekly janitorial contract. Perhaps it's a local consumer service company that requires regular vehicle maintenance and repainting for its small but growing fleet.

Whoever it is, and there may be more than one profile, you and your staff need to define it, profile it, and identify your Sweet Spot Clients. Sometimes these are not the clients who directly generate the most revenue. It may be their ability to connect you to others or the regular referrals they provide that bring you the most value. At Kids 'R' Kids Academy, we had two Sweet Spot Client profiles – parents whose relationship with us began when their child was an infant and continued for five to 11 years, and parents who entrusted us with two or more children. All of the clients were, of course, highly valued, but these are the ones we actively recruited and made certain they were consistently very satisfied.

Your Sweet Spot customers may be obvious to you as the owner, but your staff probably does not know who you most value as a client. When people working for you don't know who drives important revenue into your business, they cannot give these clients the extra-special courtesy and treatment they deserve.

I vividly remember one incident in my business that highlights this well. I was sitting in the glass-walled front office one early evening when I detected a slight "tone" in my manager's voice. I listened and watched as Mindy somewhat impatiently explain the "sick child" policy to one of our new parents. In the early childhood field, two subjects are surefire ways to get a parent's defenses up. One is money and the other is a child's illness. Land mines. Use caution.

I hopped up and came to Dad's rescue by inviting him into the office where I shared the policy and the reasons behind it. He was a brand-new father, with a brand-new baby. He hadn't yet experienced a sick child. Just because he acknowledged it on the agreement didn't mean he had read it. Or lived it. Dad was fine with my explanation and apology for the tone.

Next up, it was Mindy's turn for the office invite. I grabbed the calculator— for dramatic effect—and respectfully showed her the math. It went like this: New Dad pays $225 a week for us to lovingly care for his baby girl and expects to be treated with kindness, patience, and respect when he is here, regardless of the circumstances. In one year, New Dad will pay us more than $11,000 for this privilege. Over the course of five years, if we provide engaged, professional, and loving care for his daughter and don't insult him or otherwise lose his business, he will pay us well over $40,000. With emphasis and tone, I repeated, "Well over forty-thousand dollars." (There's that number again; weird, but true.)

New Dad was a Sweet Spot Client. I knew it, and Mindy *sort of* knew it— but it's not the same thing as when you spell it out. Message received by her and lesson learned by me. This topic went straight onto the next staff meeting agenda to be shared with all my employees.

Do you know who your Sweet Spot Clients are? Does your staff? If not, here's what I suggest. Do a first pass on your own, without input, and write down who you think your best clients are and why. Next, do some research, confirm or change your list, and add detail. Then get input from your staff and further refine your list and profile. Share this information at your next staff meeting, including *why* it's important to the business.

SWEET SPOT CLIENT EXERCISE

Who do you think are your Sweet Spot clients? Write down your ideas and reasons for including them.

1. _____

2. _____

3. _____

List five characteristics you value most in a client.

1. _____

2. _____

3. _____

4. _____

5. _____

Do the clients listed in the first list have these characteristics? What, if anything, surprises you about your findings?

_____

_____

_____

_____

_____

Sweet Spot Employee

This is your very best employee, in profiled form. This is a little bit trickier because the choices and answers may not be as obvious. There are two areas of focus: What characteristics do you value most in your employees, and which employees generate the most revenue with a consistently higher sales volume and connect well with clients? The objective behind profiling a Sweet Spot Employee is to reduce turnover within this subgroup and hire and train others to fit the profile. Turnover eats up time and drains profits. Losing a Sweet Spot

Employee usually damages hard-earned goodwill within your client base and hurts employee morale. This erodes your profit little by little.

Identifying and profiling Sweet Spot Employees is well worth the effort. It's important to make sure your management team fully understands this concept.

In your profile, use descriptive phrases like flexible, positive attitude, and detail-oriented. Consider and be specific about what those words mean to your organization. A mother of three children may not be deemed flexible, but she might have the other four characteristics you seek. What are the characteristics of the employees who generate a consistently higher sales volume or higher productivity numbers? What is a "deal-breaker" characteristic for your franchise? For example, I learned over time to not hire people who lived a certain distance away unless they also attended the local college and their work schedule complemented their school schedule. Sooner or later, and usually sooner, the commute became burdensome and expensive, no matter how much they valued the job or we valued the individual.

Knowing your profile and your "deal-breaker" before hiring new employees will help ensure you hire the best candidate, even when you or your staff are under pressure to fill positions. When you hire people, share your reasons for hiring them (and your expectations) so your team understands and learns how and why you hire Sweet Spot Employees and turn down others.

SWEET SPOT EMPLOYEE EXERCISE

Who do you think are your Sweet Spot Employees?

1. _____

2. _____

3. _____

What characteristics do you think your Sweet Spot Employees should have and why?

1. _____

2. _____

3. _____

4. _____

5. _____

Do the employees listed have these characteristics? What surprises you about your findings?

_____

_____

_____

_____

_____

Sweet Spot Community Partner

The last Sweet Spot to profile and identify is your ideal community partner. This will require some thought. The ideal partner should have specific attributes that make your investment of time, energy, and financial resources one of the more impactful decisions you make this year. In other words, don't rush this! The right partner has incredible potential for helping you strengthen your business.

I recommend you take one step back before you target a specific partner. Start by spending a few weeks to notice partnerships that have been formed in your community. This can be fascinating. I've seen Dunkin Donuts partner with LEGOLAND, Publix Supermarkets partner with multiple convenience stores, and a local smoothie franchisee partner with the YMCA. As you notice these partnerships, think about the strategy behind them, specifically the costs, benefits, and rewards for each party. Begin to think of the ideal partner as an ally and your relationship as more of an alliance than a partnership and how you can become more successful together.

I recently read the book *Originals: How Non-Conformists Move the World* by Adam Grant and found the author has a unique perspective on many of the attributes of successful people and organizations. He had this to say in Chapter 4 about Creating and Maintaining Coalitions:

"In seeking alliances with groups that share our values, we overlook the importance of sharing our strategic tactics"—in other words, learning from each other. Here are a few points I garnered from Grant's book and adapted to targeting a high-value Sweet Spot Community Partner:

- The best partners drive new clients to your business (and vice versa).
- The best partnerships have an easy-to-feel sense of shared identity and community.
- The best partners will share information, including tactics for engagement.
- The best partners add value for your existing clients.

Here are a few examples of solid Sweet Spot Community Partnerships

- **A childcare franchise partnering with the local YMCA.** Kids 'R' Kids participated in many annual children and family YMCA events, bringing staff (for face painting and games), brochures, flyers, and even enrollment forms. Reciprocally, we would send home flyers for YMCA seasonal youth sports programs and memberships, which often included exclusive discounts for our families. Periodically, a YMCA representative would be on-site at Kids 'R' Kids to register families for sports programs, saving time and money for our clients.
- **A childcare franchise partnering with the local Chick-fil-A.** Several times a year, The Cow—yes, *that* cow—would come to our lobby and hand out Be Our Guest coupons for complimentary chicken sandwiches to our parent clients and the coveted plush-toy cows for the children. Then it was our turn. Once a month, Kids 'R' Kids would manage and run the Tuesday Kids Night children's area at Chick fil-A, giving us direct access to potential new clients. Chick fil-A guests would receive a special offer from us to tour our center and register in addition to a complimentary face painting or balloon animal. It was a win-win for all parties, including staff members, who earned cash for their marketing time.

- **A national bank partnering with a national museum association.** My go-to Bank of America (BofA) ATM reminded how surprising some successful partnerships can be and why it's important to think outside the box when it comes to your Sweet Spot. Before I could get cash, BofA promoted the National Association of Museums with an ad that said as a "thank you" I could go to any of the 124 registered national museums for free the first weekend of every month. BofA gets credit for promoting a cultural experience, and museums get some much-needed new foot traffic. Pretty clever.

That's a good example of why I suggest noticing and notating partnerships for a few weeks before you make a commitment. You might be surprised how clever you really are. Think out of the box, out of your industry, and out of the franchising world. If it's way, way out there, you should run it past your franchisor first.

SWEET SPOT COMMUNITY PARTNER EXERCISE

What characteristics do you think your Sweet Spot Community Partners should have? Write down your ideas and reasons before getting input from others.

_____

_____

_____

_____

_____

List organizations and businesses you might consider or currently partner with and why they may be/or are good Sweet Spot Community Partners.

_____

_____

_____

_____

_____

Before you go on, note which partners you listed above fit some or all the characteristics. If any are existing relationships, consider how you can increase the value of the partnership so that at least three of the characteristics are met. You could start by setting a time to openly discuss what each is looking for in a partnership and build from there. You may decide to part ways if there is not enough common ground for a truly productive partnership. Certainly, that should not be considered a failure, just not ideal, which is what is required in a partnership in order to strengthen your business short term and long term.

Congratulations, you are well on your way to identifying, forming, and developing your Sweet Spots, the first step for building your Loyalty Pillar. Next, we'll talk about how to nurture these relationships and why you really need them to keep your business strong.

CHAPTER 2

Build Relationships with Customers
(and Do It Fast!)

I have always had the attitude that if you give exemplary service and stay in touch with your clients, you will have customers for life. For me, it starts from the very first purchase with a thank you postcard and a good reason to come back in and buy. The franchisor provides great marketing collateral to help us attract, build, and maintain those relationships. Finally, we "seal the deal" with a satisfaction guarantee on our products that shows we're serious about our business.

LuAnn Linker

Royal Oak, Michigan
Wild Birds Unlimited franchisee since 2001
Awarded Franchisee of the Year in 2015
Golden Eagle Club member

My franchisor, Pat Vinson, had it right when he said, "Build relationships fast." That was his advice to the new franchisees who attended training in the summer of 1998. It was only much later I fully understood what he meant and why he chose to make that point so emphatically and so early in the week.

The Stingray Boy Incident

Relationships and client loyalty are not synonymous, but they are very closely linked. There I was, thinking loyalty was all about keeping clients happy and just making sure they paid their tuition, when I nearly missed the big picture. The bigger take-away on why Building Layers of Loyalty with your clients is vital to your short-term and long-term success is that *not only* will they "keep coming back," they will actually "have your back."

Time and time again, this proved to be true: When a relationship built on loyalty and trust existed, a client problem or concern was easily addressed. If a client was new or the relationship had not been developed, a problem or concern could quickly escalate into something much worse. While client concerns are opportunities to prove our worth and grow the relationship, depending on the situation, if you have not developed a relationship, things can go south very quickly. Enter Stingray Boy.

As you're reading this story, I want you to think of the most vulnerable time of your business. That time when it's mission-critical everything goes right. Mission-critical time in the early childhood education field is, you guessed it, the first day of school.

One of our most profitable programs was the before- and after-school service, which included transportation to public elementary school in the morning and back to Kids 'R' Kids when school let out. By the time Stingray Boy had been enrolled, we were up to three buses and nine elementary schools. It was Day One of back-to-school week with all hands on deck. I was sitting in the front office when my cell phone rang. It was Susan, a former client whose two children had aged out of Kids 'R' Kids a couple of years prior to her call. Naturally, I was surprised to see her name on my phone.

> **Susan:** "Christy? Hey, this is Susan—Clay and Emma's mom." (I could hear the concern in her voice a mile away. You get good at that after a while.)
>
> **Me:** "Hey, Susan, what's going on?" (We say "hey" in the South when we know someone well.)

Susan: "Well, this is kind of weird, but I thought I should call you. There's this little boy, maybe he's around 6?... Anyway, he's in my garage now and says he's supposed to be at Kids 'R' Kids. I think he must have gotten off the public-school bus."

Me: "Oh my goodness!" (I was standing up now, waving to my manager to come in.) "Can you get his name?"

Susan said it and I repeated it for my manager, who looked it up. Sure enough, he was a new student and should have been picked up by us.

Me: "Darn it!!!!!" (Trust me, I said worse, which made Susan laugh.) "Alright, can you stay with him until I can get there? I'm walking out the door now. And Susan … thank you!!!"

As I headed to Susan's to pick up the boy, I had my manager start the investigation. Dad had enrolled his two sons on Friday. Everything was done correctly, and the boy was on the pickup list and on the list we gave to the elementary school bus monitors. Good news. Now I had to figure out how to start my phone call to Dad.

I picked up the boy and headed back to Kids 'R' Kids after assuring him he wasn't in trouble. He thought he was. That was my first clue something greater than a bus monitor was at play here. Time to call Dad.

Dad was upset (understandably) but reasonable under the circumstances. I assured him the boy's older brother was accounted for and that I would be there to meet with him and report my findings of our investigation when he arrived.

What I learned from my bus driver and confirmed myself, was that the older brother had said the boy went home sick earlier in the day. What I didn't learn, until much later, was that the younger boy was dead-set on riding the public-school bus, which was named and identified as "The Stingray Bus" because of the stingray picture on it. Kind of cute, when you think about it, right? Not so cute, according to Mom. She went ballistic and I was about to pay dearly.

Over the course of that week, I communicated daily with Dad each time the boys arrived at Kids 'R' Kids. I also changed the transportation policy. Full transparency to the parents as to why the policy changed was included in the notification as well as the urgent request they notify us immediately if their child was not going to require transportation. Of course, I let Mom and Dad know we had changed the policy to ensure what had happened to their son, who I now had privately dubbed Stingray Boy, would not happen to any other child.

Apparently, that was not enough. Not even close. Nor was waiving their tuition. Nor was my second, third, or fourth apology. Whether a friend or relative escalated this or there was something else going on in their personal life, I will never know. What I do know is that by Thursday a local news crew was at our front door demanding to hear "the story."

Off camera, I shared my side and explained what transpired and how the situation had been corrected so this would not happen again. The reporter was satisfied, he had his story, and Kids 'R' Kids was on the local channel two full news cycles for leaving a child wandering in the neighborhood. It was awful. Everyone was upset, including the owners of the other local franchises. It took days and days to finally sort everything out with all of those affected, including a not-very-friendly meeting with the school administrator whose staff had put Stingray Boy on the wrong bus to begin with even though he was wearing a yellow Kids 'R' Kids wristband.

To me, the only thing that mattered was that it could never happen again. We learned and grew and became better because of what we went through. My takeaway—and yours, too, I hope: It could have been worse. If Susan, the loyal former client, had not called me immediately, it could have been much worse. However, and this is key, if we'd had some time to get to know this family and had built a relationship, I'm betting the outcome would have been much different. Dad and Mom would have been upset, for sure, but calling the local news channel most likely would not have been their reaction.

How can I be so sure? Because over the course of fifteen years, *things happened* and some of them were pretty tough, like the child who broke his leg … twice! But we got through them by working with our clients to make things right and by improving our response and operation with each opportunity. That's why I say Pat Vinson had it right. Building relationships fast leads to loyalty and trust, and that makes all the difference. The fastest way to build client relationships is by being present, being accessible, and being appreciative.

Be Present

The simplest form of building loyalty is being present in your business. When you go out to dinner, who is the one person you notice, aside from your server? The owner or general manager. You notice good general managers because if they are present, they make sure you notice by coming by your table to check on you or standing front and center so you can't miss their presence. Here is the key: They are present *when it counts.*

LuAnn Linker, whom you met at the beginning of this chapter, learned the importance of being present and building relationships quickly as a successful Realtor. She brought those skills and instincts to her franchise when she bought an underperforming store in April 2001 and quickly recognized her Sweet Spot demographic cared about how she engaged with them. That included simple things, such as "learning their names right away and really talking to them when they come in the store."

Her skills were soon tested when our nation's most violent terrorist attack happened just a few months later and discretionary consumer spending plummeted. The relationships Linker had built in that short period of time made a big difference in her very challenging first year.

At Kids 'R' Kids Academy, I would either be in the lobby on the monthly Friday night Parent's Night Out (PNO) at drop-off time (6:30 p.m.) or I'd enjoy my Friday evening out and greet parents at pickup time (10:30 p.m.). PNO parents were generally Sweet Spot Clients, so it mattered that they saw me being present.

I also varied my schedule at the business. Sometimes I was there early (6:30 a.m.) and other times I was there at closing time (6:30 p.m.). Most of the time, however, I was there either when the majority dropped off their children or when the majority picked up. But I wasn't usually sitting in my office. For that hour, I was totally present. I talked to children and parents and walked around. Frankly, there were times it was the most pleasant and motivating part of the day. The parents did not know I might be heading to the gym or the golf course in an hour. They simply knew I was *there.*

Figure out when you can get the most out of being present in your business so you can build client loyalty *and* have a personal life. According to behavioral psychologists, the strongest reward is intermittent positive reinforcement. If you own a food service franchise, you don't need to be present every Saturday night in order to build loyalty, just every third or every other Saturday during peak hours. If you own a hair salon or other personal services franchise, you or your area manager could vary your rounds between the two or three busiest times. If your franchise model is business-to-business (B2B) or business-to-consumer (B2C), I recommend finding a way to directly connect with your Sweet Spot Clients no less than twice a year.

While your focus is on your clients, there are two significant synergies that come from this. One is that you will *engage with different staff* than you would if you kept a set schedule. The other is that because you are observing different shifts, *you'll view your operational performance through a different lens.* You may find you need more equipment or staff to grow your revenue at 8 a.m. because there is a bottleneck, or courteous service is lacking at that hour due to increased stress. The element of surprise will be uncomfortable for your staff at first, but the overall performance will rise when they cannot predict when you will be present. And hey, they'll get used to it! And respect you more for it.

Be Accessible

The best way to explain the impact of being accessible is to share an exchange that was repeated numerous times in our front lobby. A parent, usually a new parent, has a concern or issue and asks to speak to the owner. With a smile on her face, the manager would respond, "Of course. That would be Miss Christy. Her cell number and her home number are posted right over there on the front door." The client then skeptically says, "Really? Right there? You're kidding! And that's her real number?" The manager, perhaps now chuckling, "It sure is! Please tell me about your concern and I'll let her know you may be calling."

When the concern was re-stated, the manager committed to the resolution and the matter was settled on the spot. No need to call Miss Christy now!

Do you want to take a guess how many disgruntled calls I received? Maybe, *maybe* a dozen. That's it. Total. Not per year. Over the entire 15 years. I know. I find it hard to believe myself. That's why I *had* to share "Be Accessible" with you. It's too easy *not to do*. A high level of trust was built with that one simple interaction and shared information.

Here is the "client loyalty building" half of the Be Accessible strategy: The front desk manager didn't stop there. She would call or text me giving me the Who, What, Why, and the client's phone number. Within a day, I'd call the client from my cell phone during normal business hours with the facts in front of me. It was somewhat scripted and oftentimes the call resulted in my leaving a message that went very close to this: "Hi, this is Christy Delk, Miss Christy—from Kids 'R' Kids. Just wanted to touch base to let you know I'm aware of your discussion yesterday and I did confirm she (fill in the blank) so that (fill in the blank). Please do keep this number handy and feel free to call me in the future if you have anything that isn't handled to your satisfaction by my team." I kept it brief. It wasn't a social call, but I did make sure my tone was pleasant and friendly. (I want a long-term relationship after-all). Loyalty layer on top of trust layer. Done.

Be Appreciative

Eric is a surfer, salon owner and my hairstylist, who happens to be really good with highlights. (Ladies, especially those of the blonde persuasion, know how important this is.) I mean kick-ass good, and his craftsmanship gets noticed by others who are trying to stay blonde "naturally."

Over the years, I had referred at least a dozen new clients to My Guy. For years, Eric never threw me a bone. Not a complimentary blow-dry, a cut for the kiddo, nothing, nada, never. Even though my hair looked great, I recognized that I had become resentful of his lack of appreciation. As a Sweet Spot Client, I believed I should, occasionally be treated "special."

Eric and I never discussed this until after I sold the franchise and had time to seek out a secondary hairdresser. To his credit, he asked me why I had strayed. I was honest and explained as he listened intently. Today, he tangibly appreciates me regularly, much to my delight, and I'm still a loyal client. Deeply loyal. I referred him a new client just last week.

That's the kind of loyalty you want to go for in your business. Now let's figure out how you're going to do it.

Sometimes clients really stand out, maybe because they are active and positive about your business on social media or have become a great source of referrals. Their loyalty is gold to your business and should always be meaningfully thanked. It's not difficult and shows respect and courtesy in addition to gratitude. Consider a $20 or $25 gift card or certificate for your service embossed with your logo or, if appropriate, an in-kind gift from one of your Sweet Spot Community Partners. Gift cards in small denominations make showing appreciation a breeze. I kept a couple stashed in my desk drawer at all times.

I also had a stash of thank you notes and encouraged the managers to use them freely. Handwritten notes are such a rarity, and for that reason are usually greatly appreciated, but they can be time-consuming. A preprinted thank you card with a brief handwritten message works just as well. Keep the message simple and be consistent to save time. If a thank you card is what your business can support, don't worry. Your thoughtful gesture and sincere thank you will be more than sufficient to begin building loyalty.

Building Loyalty One Step at a Time

There are many ways to build client loyalty. The list below ranges in degree of difficulty, starting with the simplest to the most complex. It is in no way comprehensive. If you get an idea that is spawned from one of these, write it in the margin. Carry a notepad or have your mobile device with you for the next few months while you gather more ideas, because you will. Studies on divergent creativity, or out-of-the-box thinking, have shown we often get our best ideas when we are not at the workplace.

- **Customer survey** – Time this so you can incorporate your findings into your annual plan. Be mindful of when your clients would be more open to giving you feedback. I would not choose summer or anytime during November or December. Keep it on the short side and make sure you have a format that includes the ability to answer open-ended questions. For example, you could ask, "If you could change one thing about Kids 'R' Kids Academy, what would it be?" If the survey is done right, you will gain loyalty just for asking for feedback. Sharing the relevant results with your clients leads to deeper loyalty.

- **Thank you display or gift** – Use balloons, flowers, coffee, small treats, anything that makes a nice display, and post a sign that reads "For our valued clients" or something similar. If yours is a home-based business, mail your clients a small token—or better, drop it off personally. I once received a portfolio from a food vendor that had its 25th Anniversary seal tastefully embossed on the cover. I used until it fell apart. It was delivered by Blair Howard, the owner and son of the founder of this locally owned small business.

- **Anniversary** – The anniversary of your business should always be celebrated and used as an opportunity to build loyalty with clients and staff. Employees at Kids 'R' Kids knew what date we opened (08/23/98) and that we celebrated. We kept it simple and stress-free with a continental breakfast spread for everyone to enjoy at drop-off time and served a special cake for the afternoon and evening pickup. Some years we pulled out the grill and handed out hotdogs in the front parking lot. You bet I was present.

- **Frequent buyer promotion** – This can drive both loyalty and revenue. You know this one well. The more you commit up front, the more you save. Many personal services franchisors have adopted this strategy. As a franchisee, I recommend consulting with your franchisor before planning anything that may be deemed as diluting your brand. I used this strategy successfully during Summer Camp in order to get more than a week-to-week commitment. It was a win-win as long as the administration, check-out, and payment processes were efficient.

- **Loyalty reward program** – It's never too soon to be thinking about a program that recognizes loyalty in its most absolute form: *How long has your client been a client?* It's almost a consumer badge of honor that we all wear from time to time. "We've been eating here since it opened!" Why should we not expect the same type of prideful response from our clients in franchising? I believe we don't cultivate it as well as we should, which causes our clients to think of us as part of a bigger company or a chain and not as a local small business. A loyalty program can change that perception.

I implemented a loyalty reward program in year five of ownership and believe it helped my business stay successful for the remaining ten years. If this piques your interest, keep your mind and eyes wide open for inspiration and ideas—and take your time. This is a big step. If you are not ready to tackle a reward program, consider segmenting your clients and start small by awarding those who hit one specific milestone.

Is Client Loyalty Really That Important?

Building client loyalty is critical to strengthening your business. I want you to get this in your *bones* so your current customers will not only continue to patronize your business, they will also refer and recruit others. The ultimate? Your former clients, who no longer even *need* your service, still talk glowingly about your business because you made such a profound impression. Imagine what that type of endorsement does for your business.

I can attest to the power of that kind of loyalty; it's powerful.

And then there is this: Having to constantly replace clients is not cheap or terribly smart. It draws down your most valuable resources—your time and money—that could be much better spent. It also quietly erodes your profit margins. That's why I want to encourage you to think of the money you budget for your client loyalty program as an investment. It's very simple: Loyal clients give you the financial resources and strength to invest in finding and attracting new Sweet Spot Clients who grow your business. Not having to constantly seek out new clients gives you more time to think strategically about your business. This additional time, or "white space" leads to greater creativity, satisfaction, and motivation. That's exactly what happened to me.

I opened Kids 'R' Kids Academy in 1998. By 2002, I was thinking about what more I could do to increase revenue because the business was running at full capacity. I decided to expand on the existing property to meet the changing needs of loyal clients and my competitive advantage. Loyal clients, and my franchisor's support, gave me time to concentrate on the expansion and the confidence and wherewithal to pull it off.

Think of your loyalty investment as your path to whatever you're seeking, whether it's more time with your family, travel, or pursuing the passions you have neglected for so long. By building deep and lasting client loyalty into your program, you'll see doors open that lead to increased satisfaction and greater enjoyment in your day-to-day life and certainly more money than you ever dreamed you could earn.

Try this exercise for thinking about ways you already support client loyalty and ways you could be doing more to make clients intensely loyal to your franchise:

CLIENT LOYALTY EXERCISE

List three ways you currently show client appreciation.

1. _____
2. _____
3. _____

List three new avenues you will explore for developing deeper client loyalty.

1. _____
2. _____
3. _____

Yes, it really is *that* important. Now we'll turn to the second layer, employee loyalty.

CHAPTER 3

Show Employees You Care
(and Make It Count!)

I surround myself with a team of professionals who are also passionate about travel and encourage them to strive to make their book of business all it can be. I use a tiered pay structure so the more they grow, the more they earn. I also allow associates to log in and book their clients under a personal code so they earn the valuable travel industry award points that many owner-agents typically retain for themselves.

Alicia "Ali" Geiger

Sinking Spring, Pennsylvania
Dream Vacations franchisee since 2012
Franchisee Advisory Council member
Dream Vacations is a division of World Travel Holdings

There were many times throughout my 15 years as a small business owner that I discovered firsthand how building employee loyalty can strengthen and protect your business. It wasn't until the very end of my tenure as a franchisee that I realized loyalty and respect stretches far beyond the last paycheck.

If you have owned your franchise for even a short time, you've probably had some type of correspondence from your state unemployment agency. Maybe even a lot, as I did. Many of us employ lower-wage workers and have a fair amount of turnover. In many states, employers are responsible for a request for unemployment compensation for up to three years from the date of termination. As you probably know, it's imperative to stay on top of this in order to maintain your taxable rate as low as possible, and so I faithfully responded each month.

During the listing phase of my franchise sale, I was pretty overwhelmed. Keeping this a secret to avoid any distractions or interruptions to day-to-day operations, working double time to get the documents in order, and facing the reality of my decision had me feeling anxious and off-balance. When I received a note that an unemployment agent had left a message to call, paranoia kicked in and I assumed I had done something seriously wrong. *I had never received a call before.*

I quickly reviewed the current claims file and didn't see anything unusual and called the number. That's when it got weird. The agent politely told me she was calling to help me correct the latest documentation I had sent over *instead of denying my request.* I was a bit stunned, but went along with it. Before hanging up, I asked what had moved her to pick up the phone and to help me out. She said, using a very matter-of-fact tone, "Miss Delk, everybody here knows you give us really good documentation and your employees always tell us that you are a nice lady even when we deny their claims."

"What? You folks *know* me?" She said, "Oh yes, and I also see here that nobody has ever filed a discrimination suit against you either. Considering you own a big daycare and all, and how long you've been there, that's pretty unusual." I thanked her (again) and we ended the call.

My only reaction was a rather befuddled Seinfeld-esque, "Who knew?" And then I let that little gem of a compliment soak in. Being a consistently respectful boss with an eye to building loyalty had paid off by strengthening my business in ways I had not even considered.

It doesn't have to be big, just meaningful—something as simple as giving those you terminate a warm handshake or hug along with their last check and wishing them only the best (even if they were flat-out awful) can make a difference long after their termination. These small gestures add a protective cloak around your business, saving you countless hours, energy, and money that you can devote to strengthening your business by doing something a lot more productive and fulfilling than defending EEOC lawsuits and claims for unemployment compensation.

Mini-Ambassadors and Goodwill Gatherers

The Layers of Loyalty you build on the foundation of mutual respect will move (even former) employees to act as goodwill mini-ambassadors who refer future staff and even clients. Your reputation as a fair employer and respectful individual will precede you, protect you, and strengthen your business. And it feels a whole lot better to always take the high road. Always. No matter what.

Employee loyalty brings only good things to your business. Loyalty runs deeper than respect. To obtain this, you have to show *your* loyalty to your employees as you build additional respect and trust. It's a true symbiotic relationship. I do my part and you do yours and we'll all be better off.

Kick-Start Loyalty *This* Year—Your Unwritten Contract

After the welcome and quick agenda review, I always started the first quarterly staff meeting of the year with some version of this: "One of the things that makes us a financially healthy and secure place to work is that we value one another, and I value each one of you." Then I'd go on to state emphatically that everyone is working here for a specific reason unique to them and that I considered it my *job* to know each and every reason. All fifty of them. Fifty unwritten contracts of employment based on the respect shown simply because I understood and cared about their unique personal circumstance. I knew the reason why they were there and I wasn't going to forget it. This usually got everyone's undivided attention pretty quickly and the room quieted down.

Then, without divulging confidences, I'd prove it. By going around the room, introducing newer staff members first, I'd state why Kids 'R' Kids was a good place, or fit, for each person *this* year and add why they were a good fit for us. It was a powerful public demonstration that I fully recognized the job had to "work" for them before they could begin to work for me. I had to know and honor the reason they chose to work at my franchise. If their needs changed the following year, it might not work for them or for the business, so saying "this year" was an honest and realistic way to frame this. We all understood the contracts were also based on respect for the needs of the business *this* year.

Primarily, this kick-off was a reminder people came first at our franchise and that respect for our personal life and the work we did was a shared core value. I'd explain this in a pragmatic, yet authentic way and then we proceeded with the rest of the agenda. At that point, the whole room was intensely focused and eager to hear the plan for the year. I'd include details on how we would grow the business, where we needed to save money, and what new programs and changes would impact them directly. Sometimes they had really good things to look forward to, and some years there were takeaways and things to cut back. Regardless of the message that followed, the solid foundation of mutual respect and continued loyalty had been laid.

I realize this sounds like a pretty heavy-duty way to kick off a staff meeting, but there was plenty of humor interjected and many laughs throughout the introductions. It was most assuredly worth the time. The Loyalty Pillar was reinforced and employee loyalty was affirmed for the year. It also served as a team-building exercise. We were reminded and exposed to our differences and similarities and learned something about one another. Because it was now a shared knowledge, inside grumbling about schedules or perceived favoritism was almost non-existent. These types of issues were now viewed through a unique lens: that everyone had a place and balancing the individual needs with the needs of the business was the foundation for *our* success. *Score!*

You Don't Know if You Don't Ask

I probably skipped a year here or there, but most years I'd ask the staff to complete a survey. I would announce the Annual Survey in the biweekly employee newsletter and allowed two weeks for completion. I wanted quality feedback and set an imploring, yet positive tone about the opportunity and my need for their help. The survey covered a variety of topics, including ideas for training, benefits satisfaction and outside get-togethers. I'd ask their opinions about the management team and problems they were experiencing. I wanted to know what made them tick, what troubled them, and what would make the workplace a better place for them.

I reviewed the surveys as soon as possible to check for any critical issues. One year, the surveys confirmed I needed to terminate a key manager (we'll talk about this in **Chapter 6: "Who Is Driving the Bus?!"**, under "Responsive Leadership"). It was difficult to accept and difficult to replace her, but loyalty was taking a huge hit, and as the leader it was important for me to show I respected the opinions of staff members or take a chance of losing a lot of them that year. I didn't want to take that chance.

The surveys also helped gauge the success of employee loyalty programs for the past year, and several were booted as a result of the responses. When that happens, you get triple credit—for trying, asking, and then listening. Other surveys showed an existing program was liked and effective but needed improving. One year, we paid $50 for client referrals but it was cumbersome to track and employees sometimes had to remind the managers they were due a referral award. The survey said to keep it, so we made improvements and brought it back for another year.

When you look at your surveys, watch for job satisfaction trends, especially relating to shifts and locations. These will set the tone for how much you must do and perhaps spend this year to keep loyalty at a steady state. When unemployment hovers below four percent, reliable employees are very hard to find and keep. This is a time when you may want to introduce (additional) benefits or a floating holiday. If a new competitor is opening, keeping your team morale high is extremely critical.

If you don't currently conduct an employee survey, I recommend you try it. Here are a few suggestions:

- Keep it to ten or fewer questions, with the last one being, "What is the question I didn't ask that you wish I had?" That one is priceless. (I still use it today with students at Rollins College for extra credit.)
- Make half of the questions open-ended and you'll get more quality feedback and some great ideas. You'll want to ask questions like, "What would you like to see done differently to improve the work environment this year?" or "What benefit would you like to see added?"
- Ask respondents to note their shift and check "part-time" or "full-time." (I asked for their department and location.)
- Keep it anonymous. Some people will add their name if it's listed as optional and trust has been established. The surveys were for my eyes only, and everyone knew that.

- Communicate and commit that you will share some of the survey results within one month and then do exactly that. This helps ensure broad participation for the current and future surveys.

Only after you have organized and absorbed the responses are you in a position to plan and act on this abundance of information. Only a fool would rush in given the value of the information your loyal employees have bestowed on you, and you are no fool. *Take your time.* You have one month before you need to give feedback on the results to staff members, and of course you will do that selectively and judiciously as *you* deem appropriate for your organization *this* year. I usually included participation rates and numbers, summarized responses for open-ended questions, and then listed percentage rates or some other objective measure for other questions.

Like a good front man, you transparently "spin" the survey information to lead in a positive direction that you can impact and control. Then it's go time. You are ready to start planning by relying on the core components of Pillar 1 and build Employee Loyalty—starting with your Sweet Spot.

Design a program that targets your Sweet Spot Employee. For example, if the reliable part-time high school or college students are your Sweet Spot employees, do something that is meaningful for them. Maybe it's a contest that ties dessert sales to reward bucks for the evening shift, or a paid night off during exam week for two months of perfect attendance. Vow to consistently communicate directly to your Sweet Spots you care about their education and value their continued employment by requesting their class schedules for the upcoming semester in advance of their (usually last-minute) requests. This forces them to be more accountable in addition to the loyalty you build by being flexible for these Sweet Spot Employees. The obvious synergy is that your operation runs more smoothly and your managers learn from following your lead.

Your survey will point you in the right direction. All you have to do is ask the questions.

Keep Paychecks Positive

Payroll is more complicated today than ever, and getting paid correctly for meetings, training, and overtime helps build trust, which leads directly to loyalty. I highly recommend you stay closely involved with payroll. Even though I did not process payroll in-house, I personally submitted it to the processor biweekly. Because of that, I was able to stay on top of important personnel notes, deductions and the other things that mattered to my bottom line and that included getting payroll right for the staff.

There were two times when I turned this function over to my top manager, but I reclaimed it both times within a few months. It was not because I micromanaged or loved the task. I did not. The truth of the matter was that no one, aside from me and the person who was impacted, cared as much about getting insurance deductions right and vacation hours properly credited or deducted. Other than you, no one will be completely committed to ensuring people are *always* paid properly and that the raise that was promised was included.

You read earlier in the chapter that I avoided having a single claim by any employee relating to pay, discrimination, or other state or federal matter, and I terminated a lot of people – including one of my favorite managers who was very pregnant at the time (see **Chapter 6: "Who Is Driving the Bus?!"**, under Responsive Leadership). I attribute that to being closely involved with how people got paid, being fair when there was a decision to be made, and being timely. When a paycheck was not right, I would fix it or address it immediately. If I missed something or if something was confusing, we'd talk about it. If it was significant, I'd cut a check by the end of the day. Think of it as a "no resentment" policy, and don't plan to leave early on payroll Fridays. By Monday, resentment will have set in, and I don't mean yours. And resentment, as you know, is bad for business.

The bonus synergy here is that with your eye glued to your biggest expense, you can make immediate scheduling adjustments for cash flow purposes. The valleys are less deep and you'll sleep much better knowing that your payroll is in balance with the flow of your business revenue.

Recognition and Reward

Recognition is one of the strongest positive reinforcements that exists in the business world. According to many studies, depending on the recipient, it's even more powerful than a paycheck. As franchise owners, it's easy to ignore and to forget how meaningful it is to our staff when we personally and publicly go out of our way to heap praise for going the extra mile, meeting a program goal, or celebrating a career milestone. Many of us have part-time workers with hit-or-miss schedules that don't always line up with ours. That's why you need a fail-proof process. A systematic recognition and rewards program should keep you on the front line for the personal and public delivery, and be consistently administrated by your top manager. This will ensure your manager knows (and cares) about what is important to you. It's a process with no surprises.

One method for ensuring consistent employee recognition is through merits. There are times when an employee does something truly outstanding and a verbal "Thank you" is just not enough, especially when you are building deep loyalty. That's where merits come in.

At Kids 'R' Kids, a manager had the ability to award a merit for a variety of reasons, but one of the surest ways to receive a merit was to have a client tell a manager what a wonderful job they did. The other way was to do something in an outstanding manner that aligned perfectly with one of our quarterly objectives. For food service, it may be having a table cleaned and wiped within a set period of time after guests leave. It can be for anything you want it to be for, *and* you can and should change it up. That increases focus and engagement.

We had a small two-part form made up for just this purpose. The original went to me and the yellow copy was displayed by the recipient or tucked away for their records. Once team members had three merits, they earned four (always four) hours of paid time off (PTO). It was tabulated and awarded on the last payroll of the month and announced in the newsletter with a description of how the merits were earned. They never expired. You just needed three merits to reap the reward, and clients were delighted to know their compliments amounted to something nice for the employee. You, as the owner, will want to know when a merit is awarded so you can add your personal kudos. This combination of positive reinforcement is effective for building loyalty because it's meaningful, personal, and timely. As long as you change it up so that different behaviors are rewarded, you should be able to use this layer for two or more years.

This same form was used to document, in writing, something a staff member did that was not a serious violation or policy breech, but was not in keeping with company standards for service. A demerit was a "soft" warning—more than a verbal warning but not a formal written warning. It was a simple way to reprimand without any drama or embarrassment for the receiver. A manager simply circled "demerit" instead of "merit" and briefly described the action and ensuing correction.

Here again, you can target specific behaviors, such as not wiping down the gym equipment every night or not greeting guests consistently. If three demerits were received, then four hours of PTO were forfeited. Very rarely did anyone lose PTO hours. I cleared the slate at the end of the year because I'm a softie and wanted everyone to have a fresh start.

Like merits, demerits also worked wonders to build loyalty. You may question this, but consider employees need to see managers consistently enforcing policies, especially when you aren't present. These actions build respect and trust throughout your organization and are the foundation for deep loyalty that strengthens your business. Demerits are one way for them to easily do this.

Mix It Up

Over the years, we used a variety of loyalty programs and I believe variety was a big part of the success. We learned keeping staff engaged sometimes required something playful and unexpected such as a weeklong center scavenger hunt or ongoing trivia game with prizes. It's still work, but mixing it up helps to keep the long-term people from turning into service zombies and the new folks excited about their place of employment. That's why it's important to keep your mind and eyes wide open for ideas from other businesses and industries. Write notes and take pictures when something strikes you and ask questions. The front line of any business is usually the most forthright. Learning what other owners do within your system will also build confidence for implementing new programs and is the first place to start looking.

Permanent programs such as paid time off are important, too, and can be categorized as a benefit. I would be remiss not to highlight how important working PTO into your loyalty mix is. This one is a game-changer. Our program, fairly unique, worked like this: Every ninety days, after the first ninety days of employment, employees would receive four hours of paid time off (marked PTO) in their paychecks if they are part-timers or eight hours if they are full-timers. This was treasured gold to staff and showed I respected them enough to award time off for illness or a personal day. It also made it easier for managers to *not* grant a day off, barring a true family emergency, for someone who did not have any PTO hours. If your payroll can't support this, consider awarding PTO hours every six months or cut the awards in half with two and four hours each quarter for part-time and full-time employees respectively. You can always increase it. Vacation pay was awarded after the first year, but PTO came after 90 days. I repeat, a game-changer and well worth it.

One other specific program that made a huge impact was forming marketing teams. Only employees in "good standing" (which was defined) could apply. These formal mini ambassadors would sign up for marketing events outside of the normal workday and visit community partners and other prospects during the work day when we could cover for them. Marketing was an opportunity to change one's work pace and earn extra money. We also had a team program, as a reward for being in good standing, for a monthly Friday night event at the center, Parents' Night Out. Members of both teams were known for being highly trusted and valued employees by me and the rest of the staff.

Here is the list of topics I used for brainstorming loyalty programs throughout the years. I'd love to hear from you and learn about the programs you use that made a difference in your franchise, and those you thought would be winners, but bombed. I've had plenty of those, too. Write me at Christy@ChristyWilsonDelk.com.

- Paid conference fee and lunch-and-learns
- Benefits, such as 401(k), health, dental, life; and paid time off
- Memberships (fitness, shopping)
- Short-term loans

- Employee and client referrals
- Off-site social meet-ups
- Themed events and parties
- Anniversaries, birthdays, career milestones, retirement
- Personal and family information programs (retirement, college savings, health improvement)
- Financial education information programs (mortgage process, credit unions/banking, saving)
- Owner surprises (coffee bar, ice cream social, raffle drawings)

Please don't let this list intimidate you. Donuts, ice cream, pizza, and potlucks were the highlights in my early years and are a franchise staple. Every franchise, every year, and every single budget is unique. Sometimes revenue hits a plateau and programs get cut back or cut altogether. Even if you have a very small budget, or are unsure what kind of budget you have for this effort, do something to build employee loyalty. The worst thing you can do is *nothing*.

Start Now

Doing nothing does exactly nothing for your business. If you are serious about making your organization stronger, this is for you. A note of caution: The second-worst thing you can do is start an employee loyalty program and then let it die a slow death by not promoting it until it gets traction. That creates uncertainty in your ranks, and uncertainty chips away at the Strategic Leadership Pillar.

When you kick off a new program, I recommend conducting a quick intake as you make your rounds. You may need to beef it up if enthusiasm is lacking. Announce the changes and then take another read. At the end of the year, make the decision to keep it, fix it, or cut it. Even if the next one bombs, your staff knows you tried something unique, and you *do* get (loyalty) points for that. But it won't. You learn each time and you're smart.

It's time to commit to growing your business by building a strong Loyalty Pillar. It doesn't matter if you are reading this in April, July, or October. You can start building loyalty *this* month by beginning with something small. Your employees will notice what you do and will be immediately delighted. Over time, they will reward you through their loyalty. And *that's* very good for your business and your bottom line.

EMPLOYEE LOYALTY BUILDING EXERCISE

Spend a few minutes and answer the following questions:

Think about what you do now, if anything, to kick off your year. Does it have the impact you need to accomplish your plans this year? If not, what ideas do you have now that would be more impactful?

_____

_____

_____

_____

_____

List the top three things you think your employees value most about working at your franchise.

1. _____
2. _____
3. _____

List three quick and easy ways you can start building loyalty in the next thirty days.

1. _____
2. _____
3. _____

Now that we've thoroughly covered building Layers of Loyalty for clients and employees, only two more remain: building loyalty in your community and with your franchisor. Don't stop now! You are more than halfway through this section, and this is a critical investment in your business.

CHAPTER 4

Connect with Your Community

Barbeque to the Rescue came out of an ongoing franchisor program called Random Acts of BBQ. What we do locally is find organizations that do really good things for others, like first responders, hospice, Feeding America, Ronald McDonald House, Fisher House for Veterans, and hospital employees, and tell them we are going to bring them a free meal just to say thank you. Our goal is to inspire others in our community and our own staff to give back, and it's a way to thank all of our customers. They have empowered us and allowed us to take what we make and share it with others in our community.

Edward "Eddie" Titen

Clearwater, Florida
A licensed franchisee of Sonny's BBQ since 1998
Multi-unit owner and president of the
Franchise Cooperative Owners Group since 2013

One of the biggest mistakes franchisees make is not becoming a part of their local community. In the past, franchisors did not emphasize community engagement as a top priority and some believe it hurt the industry. The good news is, it's changing fast with initiatives like Franchises Give Back through the International Franchise Association (IFA) and other public outreach and education programs developed by IFA leadership.

These programs are designed in part to broaden the industry profile as major economic contributors and underscore the importance of connecting with your community as local small business owners. Many franchisors have aligned with national organizations and are having a positive impact in communities all over the country. One takeaway: Being engaged with your community is good for the industry, your brand, and you as a franchisee. Being active, building connections, and giving back to your community will go a long way toward ensuring your long-term success.

Case for Connecting

When I wrote this chapter, Eddie Titen stayed in the forefront of my mind as a franchisee who embodies what it means to truly connect with your community. Eddie is a longtime friend and a long-term Sonny's BBQ franchisee who leads by example from the front line. What Eddie does for his community and his franchise system has earned him numerous franchise awards, television interviews, and no doubt some increased revenue over the years. It works because his motives are pure and his passion for giving back is genuine. With Eddie, it's all heart, and it shows.

Building community loyalty is critical for strengthening your business. This loyalty layer will help you:

- Create a **true competitive advantage** when you form community partnerships and relationships because your competitors will, in all likelihood, not.
- Get low-cost **exposure, publicity, and goodwill** that will attract new clients and staff through direct contact and referrals, decreasing your marketing and recruiting costs.
- **Earn deeper respect and trust** from your clients and staff, which leads to deep loyalty.
- Exude **leadership** qualities that transcend being the owner/operator of a franchise.
- Better **protect your business** during economic downturns, tight employee markets, and potential negative publicity.

I want you to become known and recognized as a small business owner who cares about your community. Done right, this will benefit you almost immediately and will become foundational for building your Loyalty Pillar. Doing what small business owners have been doing for generations is one of the best, low-cost and high return strategies you can develop. The perspective you gain when you are helping others will remind you that what you do is important. And others will notice. Your local involvement can turn into a great employee loyalty and team builder. That's exactly the kind of synergy you will come to expect as you continue to build your 4 Pillars.

Build Your Outreach Strategically

Of course, I don't recommend you jump into this without a plan. There are many ways to connect your franchise with your community. I suggest you be strategic in order to maximize the benefits. Start by looking at your options before you make a commitment.

A strategic community outreach should:

- Align as much as possible to your service and brand.
- Be inexpensive to implement, especially if you are a newer franchisee.
- Not take you away from your operation for an inordinate amount of time.

Here are a few low-investment ways to consider connecting with your community. These are applicable to almost all segments. Be sure to write down any new ideas that come to mind in the chapter exercise as you plan your loyalty-building strategic community engagement program.

1. **Become a board member for a nonprofit**, especially if it aligns with your core business.
   - **Advantage:** This can get your name out in the community while you're doing something good to give back. Most associations promote their organizations, and generally that includes posting a list of current board members on their websites.
   - **Investment:** Zero dollars.
   - **Time:** Approximately two hours a month.

- **Example**: The owner of a pet care franchise could volunteer on the board of a local rescue or shelter.
- **How to get started:** Call or write to the board chair or the organization's director.
- **Suggestion:** Volunteer for the organization for a few hours before you inquire about the process of getting onto the board. This will give you insight into how the organization operates and whether it is a good fit for your service, and it will allow the organization to get to know you.

2. **Write educational articles for local publications**.
   - **Advantage:** These are widely distributed and can be free publications that clients and prospects pick up at various locations or see when they are delivered to homes or posted online.
   - **Investment:** Zero dollars.
   - **Time:** Approximately two hours to write a good article of 300 to 500 words on a topic that interests your clients and prospects.
   - **How to get started:** Call or write to the publishers to highlight your expertise and pitch a few topics. They might want to see a writing sample.
   - **Suggestion:** Ask someone you know who has solid language and grammar skills to read the article and offer feedback before you send it to the publication.

3. **Volunteer at community events.**
   - **Advantage:** Donating your time at an event can give your business and your staff maximum exposure. For example, a visiting care services franchise could volunteer at the annual American Cancer Society walk or form a team to go through the course. Your team should consist of you and a few bright, cheery, and knowledgeable staff members.
   - **Investment:** Whatever the event costs to sponsor. This can range from a hundred dollars for a six-foot table or more for an outdoor

booth to a few thousand dollars for inclusion on all of the marketing materials and event signage.

- **Time:** This will vary depending on the event, but you can ask staff members to get involved with you and keep your own time to a minimum. This also gives your employees an opportunity to shine outside the normal scope of their work.

- **How to get started:** Look for opportunities in your community by asking your team, your customers, and your friends whether they can alert you to upcoming events that might fit your mission.

4. **Join a networking association** such as the local chamber of commerce or a service organization like Kiwanis or Rotary Club.

- **Advantage:** The smaller the organization, the more impact you can have by joining. This is ground zero for positioning yourself as a small business owner who cares about the local community. Additionally, a chamber membership often provides educational and networking events, and you can send your up-and-coming managers. As your franchise becomes more involved, you will receive client and staff referrals from other members.

- **Investment:** Usually $100 to $300 a year in membership dues, often based on the number of employees in your franchise. After that, the networking events are minimal costs and your staff will enjoy going when you can't attend. You will receive a sticker or plaque to place at the entrance of your business, and you can use the logo in your marketing material.

- **Time:** Usually one to three hours a month.

- **How to get started:** Look up the contacts for your local chamber or service club online and reach out to ask how to join.

5. **Volunteer as a speaker** for professional and industry organizations that welcome guest presenters with knowledge in the field. You can also volunteer to speak at local chambers and service clubs that hold regular meetings for their members.

- **Advantage:** When you help others in the community by sharing your expertise, audience members share that knowledge with their friends, neighbors, and other business people. This presents you as an expert and serves as a source of referrals. Additionally, you will leave feeling motivated yourself.
- **Investment:** Zero dollars.
- **Time:** Typically, one to two hours of preparation time and one to two hours to attend and present.
- **How to get started:** Reach out to people you meet in the community and let them know you are available for speaking engagements about your field of expertise. If you don't tell them, they won't know.

STRATEGIC OUTREACH EXERCISE

Now it's your turn to brainstorm your ideas. Think for a few moments about your clients. Are they other small business owners, elderly couples, pet owners? Are they health-conscious, family-focused, concerned about their appearance? Write down the demographics that best describe the majority of your clients.

_____

_____

_____

Now, focus on your Sweet Spot Client. Write down any additional important demographics such as income level, more narrow age group, or specific distance from your business.

_____

_____

_____

Last, think about their lifestyle. What do they do during their non-work hours? Where do go? What organizations do they join? Do they read a local entertainment publication, lifestyle magazine, or college newspaper? Attend health fairs, go on bar crawls, or shop at the Farmers Market? Go wide and deep here.

_____

_____

_____

_____

_____

Refer to the work you did here when you are ready to fine-tune this to connect strategically to your community. This will help you achieve the maximum benefit for your investment of time and money because you will be better aligned to attract the type of clients you most desire.

Once you've developed this area of loyalty, you will be among the minority of franchisees who understand that a reputation as a local small business owner who cares about the community leads to a stronger business and a stronger cash flow. Not to mention, some truly excellent sleep.

Just one more loyalty target left: your franchisor. There's a reason I saved it for last. Keep reading! You're almost there.

CHAPTER 5

Forge Franchisor Loyalty

In order to be truly successful, I believe you need a strong relationship with your franchisor and to believe in not only the concept and the business model, but also the franchisor's philosophy. There's no doubt that the loyalty and relationship I've built with my franchisor has presented me with opportunities to grow that I might not have had otherwise.

Bill Pyle

Denver, Colorado
Freddy's Frozen Custard and Steakburgers franchisee since 2007
Co-owns 11 Freddy's in the Denver area and is developing
several more in Orlando, Florida, and Birmingham, Alabama

Many of us find our way to franchise ownership because we were downsized, laid off, right-sized or fired. Some, myself included, could check "all of the above." We're a bunch of corporate ex-pats who, in many cases, were not terribly enthusiastic about the politics and policies that often came with the territory. With franchise ownership, we hoped, a lot of that would go away.

Here's a news flash: It *kind of* did—just not how you were thinking, or perhaps hoping, it would. It's not the same type of politics we experienced in the corporate world and it may take some time if you're new before you understand where the lines are. It's a different business model, as we know. We're partners, but we're not. We're owners, but we don't have carte blanche decision-making powers. Some franchisors micromanage and others are hands-off as long as you pay your royalties on time and generally toe the line.

Our industry runs the gamut from founders and families running the day-to-day to brands that are owned and managed by investment partnerships or corporations. You may have signed your agreement with the founder and now your partner is the board of directors at an investment company. It can get messy and complicated, but it doesn't have to.

When you made your decision and the paperwork was signed, you became part of the family for the next five to 30 years depending on your agreement. Like a marriage, we don't usually see the less-appealing aspects of the family until after the kiss has sealed the deal. Every franchise system has its quirky uncle and family dysfunctions, and yours does, too. Focusing on the dysfunction won't get you where you want to go. Even if the family structure changes; you're still married. Your goal is to enjoy the benefits of the relationship and make all the money you can. That means you need to have a positive and productive relationship with your franchisor. That's the loyalty and the politics that Bill Pyle, who I met on a Southwest flight to Denver, is talking about. Bill's ownership group is one of the most successful franchisees in the Freddy's system, and he pointed directly to his relationship with his franchisor when asked about the source of his success. Many top-tier franchisees will tell you the same.

That's why I put building Franchisor Loyalty last.

Franchise founders are entrepreneurs in their purest form. Their inspiring stories help us to believe in ourselves and in what they have created. This purely American-born business model has given many entrepreneurs around the globe the opportunity to own a business and they want you to be successful. For most, it's not solely about the money. Relationships matter to them. Your relationship with them matters a great deal. After all, *you're family now.*

Loyalty Leads to Recognition

When I remember to include it, I pray for humility. When I owned my franchise, I liked to be recognized and I loved it when my franchisor dished it out. I can't help it. Like many franchisees, especially those of us who came from corporate jobs, we are conditioned to being commended for good numbers, good work, and improvements to our business. Plus, we're competing with other family members, and any form of public recognition just feels good. This kind of attention, however, is about more than your ego. It's also good for your business. And that starts with quality and service, not politics.

Once you've gotten established, if you don't maintain a healthy dialogue with your quality assurance or customer service team, the front line of your franchisor, chances are your franchise is not going to garner any commendations anytime soon. The dialogue includes following system processes, sending royalties on time, and receiving consistently good marks on your quality reports. It also means you need to be present when someone from corporate visits. That means making yourself available, even when the visit is an unannounced inspection—if only for a few minutes, to show engagement and respect.

Once your reputation for adhering to processes, consistent quality and professional communication has been established, you will start to receive recognition from your franchisor. The special and unique things you do that enhance current franchise processes will be shared throughout the system and held up as examples of what others could do. When you show steady revenue growth, receive consistently high marks on franchise quality reports and pay your royalties in a timely manner, you are being an upstanding family member. Franchisors usually recognize those members with a plaque or certificate as tangible proof you are a highly valued, successful franchisee.

That tangible proof should be displayed front and center. When people enter your place of business, they need to see your certificates and plaques. Any new designation or award should be included on proposals for service, new signs on vehicles, and updated business cards. Achievement designations will help you earn new clients, hire better employees, and receive positive publicity. Your existing clients will know you are a highly valued franchise that cares about customer service and quality when they learn of your achievement. Client and staff loyalty grows deeper when you share something very positive about your business and it gives them bragging rights.

The recognition you receive from your franchisor matters to those who matter to you.

Loyalty Leads to Access

Many of us fled the corporate scene because we didn't care for the politics or we weren't good at playing the game, or in my case, both. Franchisor loyalty is not so much about politics as it is about aligning deeply with your common goals: *You both want to make money and enjoy your time while doing it.* Aligning and accomplishing those two goals requires you generally get along well with people in order to have a mutually beneficial productive relationship. That's not politics, it's just being smart.

For most, a big part of your long-term satisfaction is going to be directly proportionate to the willingness of your franchisor to take a "hands-off" approach. As entrepreneurs and owners, that's just who we are, and your franchisor understands you prefer minimal feedback. In the beginning of your tenure, while you are "learning to walk," it will be different.

There will probably be more oversight than you may like, but you know you need it and accept it. If you play by the rules, build your revenue, and have a positive attitude toward the franchise organization, it won't take long before you have crossed over and are walking tall. Your attitude is reflected by how you relate to your assigned quality assurance representatives, fulfill requests (usually for information) in a timely manner, and pay your royalties consistently and on time. If you are a good spokesperson for future franchise owners and occasionally mentor, you will then be off and running with more confidence because you have earned your franchisor's favor. That's where you want to be. Mutual trust, respect, and loyalty are firmly intact. You know your role and your franchisor can count on you to play it consistently.

At this level, you have access. Access to information, access to influence, and access to exceptions and opportunities. For me, this was best demonstrated in 2002 when I was considering a major expansion.

Access Leads to Approvals and Success

I had decided the time was right, even if I wasn't quite ready to deal with new construction and all the permitting hurdles and stress that come with it. I had been at capacity for a couple of years and was worried about staying competitive.

Several new competitors were sniffing around and one had already announced. I had to act now if I wanted to secure my advantage long-term.

The expansion project would be a second building approximately 9,000 square feet located directly behind the main center. I had the very good fortune to buy a larger land parcel than franchisees usually secure and at a very good price because of the peculiar zoning. (It was zoned for a church but churches apparently need more than 3.5 acres. The neighbors were worried something far worse than a children's center might be forced on them if they didn't approve the zoning change request, and the land owner was tired of dealing with the neighbors). The bottom line was I had well over the required minimum of 1.25 acres for building a new facility. To my knowledge, no one else in the system had done anything like this and I had no idea how to predict the outcome. All I needed to get started on my expansion plans was my franchisor's approval.

I took a deep breath and called my franchisor, Pat, to tell him what I had in mind. His big concern was that I was "biting off more than I could chew" because he "loved me like a daughter" and didn't want to see me get into something that was going to be too much for me. First, he meant that about the daughter thing; the man was incredibly familial. And second, I was one of the very few franchisees who did not have a spouse or partner running the business with them. He was right to be worried. Pat was on his plane and down to see me within a few days. The man was extremely busy, but I can't remember a single time when he did not take my call on his cell phone or come to my center if I needed him. Ever.

We walked the property and I told him my vision for the Enrichment Center and my desire to make it feel more like a campus. Voluntary pre-kindergarten was about to break loose in Florida and this new suburbia had no church-sponsored preschools for part-time students. The need for non-full-day programming was great. I told him about the slew of competitors that were ready to break ground and convinced him I could handle it. He nodded and said, "OK, then, Shug, how are we going to do the driveway?" He proceeded to tell me how it would work best to lay it out. The man was pure genius about configuring building footprints to work on just about any land track. He knew what he was doing and was willing to share his time and knowledge with me. That kind of access to that level of experience and wisdom is priceless.

The Enrichment Center became the crown jewel of my operation. It allowed me to make more money than most of the other franchisees in the system and kept me super engaged with my business for the next several years. Like Bill Pyle, I achieved this success because of my loyalty to my franchisor and his loyalty to me. Our relationship was based on mutual respect, trust, and shared goals.

Loyalty Leads to Wisdom

Franchisees don't like to ask for help. We're proud people. I know it and you know it. So does your franchisor. When I look back, one of the things I would have done differently was to ask for help more often because, in hindsight, whenever I did, it turned out very well. Like young adults, we often don't ask until we've gotten in trouble or we're stuck on a problem and can't find a solution. I was no different.

That crown jewel I just told you about? It almost did me in. Until I called Pat—again. He probably answered on the second ring with his standard, "Hey Shug, whatcha got?" What I had was a near-empty building and a big fat mortgage and an increased payroll that my enrollments were not supporting. I was not sleeping well, I was definitely not having fun, and I was freaking out on the inside by the time I finally called. What he didn't say is as important as what he said. He didn't say, "I was afraid of that." What he said was, "I'll see you by the end of the week."

By Friday afternoon I had a new plan. It took Pat about fifteen minutes to walk around the center, look at a few numbers, and tell me what I needed to change. It was so easy I'm almost embarrassed to tell you what he said. And he was right. It worked. All it took was one phone call, one walk around the center, and some jet fuel, and my newly expanded business was set for nine years of steady growth and handsome profits. That was the last time I hesitated to pick up the phone and ask for help.

No matter how well you think you know your business and your local market, your franchisor probably has a solution for your problem. Or someone on his or her corporate team does. They've been exposed to a lot more that works and doesn't work. It's as simple as that. But you have to ask.

By the way, what Pat told me to do was to stop limiting myself. I was fixated on the Enrichment Center being a part-time program that was a feeder to Pre-K and after-school. "Shug, I don't know why you don't just make this an expansion of your full-day program and let those part-time children go home to their mamas and keep the others there until their parents pick them up after work. That's what you should be doing here. I know you had your mind set on what you wanted it to be, but you need to change your mind if you want to fix this." And that's what I did. My ego had gotten in the way of seeing the solution. Pat cleared the way for me.

Loyalty Leads to Deep Loyalty

Franchisors understand the rigors of being a business owner. Most of them did it themselves before you ever heard about them. They know you are going to have the occasional employee who is going to say or do the wrong thing, generating a complaint call to the home office or an ugly social media post. They also know you are not going to score perfect reviews every time and that you do not want to be on-site every hour of every workday. However, they are not going to be able to look past those things if you have not developed a track record, shown appropriate respect for the system, and allowed them to get to know you and your values and ethics. This takes time and perhaps, like me, letting go of some of your ego or inhibitions.

Even if you are a private person and "business is business," allowing your new family to really get to know you will feel pretty good over time because you'll know they trust you, respect you, and have your back. I recall one day sharing some of the heartache regarding raising my son, Roland, with a corporate quality assurance representative. It had been a particularly tough week, including a call from his principal to come pick him up. (Roland was "expended"—his word for expelled and suspended.) I came back to work and had obviously been crying. The QA rep stopped what she was doing and for the next thirty minutes we talked about the difficulties of balancing work and family and how amazed they all were that I could run a Kids 'R' Kids Academy by myself. I'll always remember that conversation, because it was the first time I really felt the care and concern about me personally. It wouldn't have happened had I not opened up.

A huge weight came off. I didn't have to be perfect and neither did my franchise. I learned an important lesson that day about letting the franchisor-franchisee relationship *happen*. I also learned that if I was loyal to them, they would be loyal to me.

I tested them mightily throughout the years. Two times I had a news crew at my front door. On several occasions, I called to inform them a state licensing agent was coming by because a disgruntled parent had called in a serious complaint. Most of those were unfounded, but at least a couple were not. It didn't matter. They always had my back. And I had theirs.

Be Loyal to Your Franchise Family

You've seen why it's important for your business to build and maintain Layers of Loyalty with your franchisor and its corporate office team. How do you show respect and forge a deeper relationship? It's not as difficult as you might think. There are things I recommend you should commit to, or at least try your best to do.

Always do:
- **Pay royalties on time or call.** Generally, within ten days of the due date is acceptable. If you do not have an automatic deduction in place, and you pay your bills twice a month, then half of the payments will be well within the generally accepted grace period. If you are having a cash flow crunch or traveling for an extended period, make a courtesy call so your franchise accounting person is aware.
- **Be present.** Being on-site during a visit of any kind shows respect for the franchisor. If you cannot be present, a personal call from you explaining why you will not be available will be greatly appreciated. Sometimes it's painful to be present if an inspection takes a full day. Take a break and come back to review the notes and see your "family" off properly.
- **Pay a visit.** Once every couple of years, I would go to the corporate office. I called several days in advance and didn't stay long, but occasionally had lunch with one of the key personnel and always had some face time with the owners. It meant a lot to the corporate staff and, by extension, the

franchisor. I knew this, because invariably someone would say they were sorry they missed me when I stopped in. I almost always left with some "freebie" promotional item or intel about something that had not been announced yet.

- **Congratulate them.** Franchisors care about milestones. Growing a franchise system is extremely difficult, so it's appropriate and appreciated for you to send a congratulatory note or gift basket when your franchisor reaches a strategic goal such as the 200th unit or is now in every state. Anniversaries are also cause for celebrating. I recall sending a bonsai plant for the 25th anniversary celebration. It was sitting on the reception desk the next time I stopped in.

- **Notify them.** Anytime there is an inkling of something serious brewing, call the appropriate person at corporate and send an email confirming the conversation. Being communicative up front is effective for two reasons. You are in control of the story and you can ask for advice or recommendations. Score and score. I trained my managers to do this if I was traveling and not available. It deepens all of the relationships. If your managers are running the business in your absence, they will get trusted advice. This happened when we had a (small!) fire and I was in Europe. Karen, the manager, handled the crisis and then called corporate to see what else she should do. She was reassured by the ensuing conversation and received excellent advice about communicating with the parents quickly, before they heard from their child later that there had been a fire at school that day. (*Not good.*)

Commit to:
- **Offer your experience.** Once you are established, it's time to offer your service as a mentor or advisor for new franchisees. This does not mean you will always be willing or able to serve in this capacity, but rather that *this* year, you would like to contribute in this way. Offer your service, state your time frame, and copy the franchisor or CEO so your offer is noticed. I was informally mentored by a franchisee across town. Judy

Manella was a lovely woman and a generous mentor. I learned a lot from her and will always be grateful.

- **Offer your time.** If you are a franchisee in good standing or are trying to improve your relationships at corporate, offering your time in whatever capacity is needed will be appreciated. Often, the franchisor needs early stage development feedback from franchisees on new service concepts, pricing structures, or operational changes such as testing new software. Fielding phone calls from prospective franchisees is another way to offer your service of time. Again, set a limit and time frame to this offer. Up to two calls a month for one year is a good place to start. See how it goes and if you were effective before you re-commit.

- **Offer your service.** Serving on the Franchise Advisory Council (FAC) is both an honor and a higher level of commitment. That said, there is probably no greater way to show your loyalty and dedication for your system than being on the FAC. I am a believer in the adage that "You get what you give," and based on what I've learned from seasoned industry people, this is no truer than when one serves on an FAC or other franchise system forum.

- **Offer your franchise.** Prospective franchisees benefit greatly from visiting a franchise that's fully operational or, for home-based franchises, working side-by-side for a day. Offering to provide a tour or allowing prospects to shadow you earns you a gigantic gold star in your franchisor's book. I found, as an interesting side benefit, that it also rekindled my appreciation for what I had accomplished. I toured two centers before making a buying decision. I realized much later that they may have been "paying it forward," and so tried to do the same.

- **Offer your facility or home.** Hosting training or meetings is another way to show your appreciation and build loyalty. If your franchise or home is centrally located to neighboring franchises, this is an easy way to do something meaningful for the franchisor and for your local franchisees. This was the case for my franchise, and we hosted many training workshops. As much as my hosting was appreciated, I believe my staff and I were the greater beneficiaries because no one had to go out of their way to participate and they enjoyed showing other staff around "our" school. Another loyalty win-win.

If you are not comfortable offering your experience, time, or location for training, then it may be too soon in your ownership cycle or simply not the right year to take on something extra that is going to expose you and your business in this way. I fully understand that and think it's completely reasonable. If, however, it's neither of those, then I strongly recommend trying to figure out what is holding you back from occasionally contributing in this way. If there is resentment being harbored or some other serious issue, try to flush it out and have a heart-to-heart with your representative or franchisor about it. Getting the conversation started is a great step toward finding the passion and joy of business ownership you truly deserve. Holding back will not get you any closer to what you desire.

Your relationship with your franchisor is extremely important to you and your family's overall well-being, and your franchisor should always value and respect your desire to improve it. The mere fact you are reading this book shows that you strive for improvement and are willing to grow personally and professionally. Based on that, I can assure you that your opinion will be valued.

One last thing. I called the Kids 'R' Kids Academy corporate office last week to finalize permission for referencing them in my adventures. Want to guess what the second question was? That's right,

"How's Roland doing?" Nancy, the long-time company receptionist, asked about my son.

Good to know I'm still family.

You have strengthened and fortified your business with layer upon layer of loyalty with clients, employees, your community, and your franchisor family. Now it's time to focus on *you*. Are you ready to lead?

┌─────────────┐
│ *Pillar 2* │
└─────────────┘

STRATEGIC LEADERSHIP

Protect Your Business

P lease do correct me (email please!) if I'm wrong. Before you bought your franchise, all you could think about was making this franchise dream a reality. Becoming a business owner, and the confidence and excitement that reality generates, is enthralling. During your onboarding and franchise training period, a barely audible whisper of judgment or self-doubt may have crept in, but you brushed it aside and powered through. Not everyone can do what you did, and that accomplishment says a lot about your strength of character and drive to succeed. Congratulations, *you did it!*

Now that you have what you wished for, the stakes are higher and the whisper, at times, is a much louder voice. For most, me included, owning and operating a franchise is significantly more challenging than we anticipated and probably more than we care to admit to. Being a franchise owner can be unnerving and even scary at times— like when cash flow is low, the quarterly tax bill is due, and you just realized one of your best or favorite clients hasn't been in for a while. There were plenty of nights, especially in the early years, when I would have trouble falling asleep thinking about a particular problem or a more existential, "What if this *doesn't* work?" After the first expansion, I really questioned myself about how I approached my business as a leader and how I could better protect it going forward.

Take comfort in knowing most successful franchisees have occasional moments of doubt including those in the top tier of your system and seasoned multi-unit owners. It's part of being a leader. If you asked, they would probably tell you that *how* you lead through the challenges, invest your leadership time, and manage the day-to-day is what will protect your business over the long-term. How you lead will help you stand out in your local market as both a good employer and a good businessperson who cares about the local community—which leads directly to goodwill. Goodwill is the cloak that helps protect your business from the known and unknown elements and valleys that cause harm and instability.

How you achieve that high level of goodwill and have the time to move your business forward requires a leadership strategy. Pillar 2, Strategic Leadership, is about big-picture thinking and breaking it down into actionable layers so none of it is overwhelming and your leadership capital and energy are used most effectively. After all, you are just one person with one great big job. Strategic leaders know when to *go big* and when to *let it go*. Going big with leadership allows you to truly enjoy your ownership time and make plans to accomplish more with your existing franchise or make plans to buy another unit. It gives you the confidence and assurance that you are well-positioned to make your planned profit this year and have the stability built in to be successful long-term.

Strategic leaders don't always start with what is expected. When it comes to leading your organization, I recommend you start by preparing for the unexpected. Unexpected moments of potential crisis represent some of the greatest challenges you will face as an owner.

If you can lead through the unexpected—and you *can*—then you can lead through anything.

CHAPTER 6

"Who Is Driving the Bus?!"

Before anyone starts working at one of my stores, I share my philosophy: "If I take care of the employees, the employees will take care of the clients and the clients will take care of the business. That means I want you to be the very best version of yourself personally and professionally, because ultimately, that's good for me." If the person responds positively, then I know I have a good candidate.

Rob Krecak

Milwaukee, Wisconsin
uBreakiFix franchisee since 2014
Multi-unit, multi-brand (Anytime Fitness) franchisee

Traditional leadership books, speeches, and training programs focus on the attributes of strong leaders and how they inspire and motivate their organizations. This is not that kind of book. As you now know, I'm more of a hands-on kind of leader and submit that you probably are, too. Franchise owners have to be. It's a fast-paced environment with barely enough time to switch hats some days.

Rob Krecak is totally transparent about his motivation and strategy for developing his teams. He doesn't have time to mess around and gets right to the point in candidate interviews. It's good for those who make the cut and it's great for his business. More specifics about Rob's strategy later in the chapter. It's win-win, inexpensive, and very cool. Like Rob.

Few leadership books talk about when to use different leadership strategies. Knowing and recognizing when to use a specific strategy can have a huge impact on how quickly you resolve a problem and how you move your business forward successfully in a given year. I break it down like this:

1. Unplanned Leadership – What will you do when the unexpected (and sometimes the unthinkable) happens?
2. Responsive Leadership – How will you respond to the opportunities (sometimes disguised as challenges) that present themselves?
3. Planned Leadership – Do you have an intentional, deliberate plan for how you will lead key stakeholders this year?

The objective is to help you identify and properly lead through each of these three categories so your customers, staff, and community recognize you as a strong leader and want to associate with you, do business with you, and refer others to you. This combination of leadership strategies is what protects your business short-term *and* long-term.

Unplanned Leadership

One of the greatest opportunities for you to display leadership is by what you do when the unexpected happens. This is your chance to step up—and one you don't want to miss, however unnerving it may be.

I read an article last year in *Franchise Times* about the owner of a restaurant franchise. She walked into her restaurant on Father's Day to check on things and enjoy breakfast with her husband, and the next thing she knew, she was cooking—for the entire day. Her lead cook had walked off the job on one of the busiest days of the year *and there was no one else to do it*. She handled it beautifully and reported that, although her leadership was tested, the end result was that she had earned the deep respect of her staff and clients.

Will you be ready when a situation calls for Unplanned Leadership? Will you recognize it for what it is and seize the moment? It may come when you least expect it.

My leadership was tested very early in my ownership days. Here's my favorite Unplanned Leadership story:

It was a Friday afternoon late in the fall of 1998. I opened my Kids 'R' Kids Learning Academy franchise in August and things were going well. That is, until Alex walked in. Alex was my guy. My "go-to" employee. I recruited him several months before I opened, and he was an integral part of the operation. He drove the bus, performed maintenance duties, and was a team leader for the before- and after-school program.

Alex had bad news. Really bad news. Friday was his last day. *Today* Friday, not "two weeks from now so I might have time to find his replacement" Friday. Another (non-franchised) center owner, closer to home, offered him a job he couldn't refuse, and he was to report on Monday. I never saw it coming.

I went to my director and told her what had just happened. Panic swept through the office. Deer in the headlights panic. Who was going to drive the bus on Monday? A driver for any early childhood program has to be screened and properly documented to meet Florida regulations. This was not a "Just hire a bus driver off the Internet" type of problem.

I had planned to get my commercial driver's license (CDL) for emergency short-term situations. But over the weekend? The full licensing process normally takes at least two weeks, allowing time for testing, practicing and basic mechanical knowledge. I had to act quickly. I grabbed my oversized working-mom purse, looked over my shoulder, and said, "I've got this" as I headed out the front door. It was 2 p.m., and the Department of Motor Vehicles office closed at 5. I would run through the options and figure out a plan on the way there. My first hurdle was obvious: Could I take the written CDL test and obtain a learner's permit *within the next three hours?* I'd never even looked at a book. I repeated, "I've got this" to myself.

As I focused on the next hurdle, assuming I passed all three components of the written test and received a learner's permit, how could I get licensed to drive by 7 a.m. Monday morning? I knew this was just the beginning of a very long weekend.

It was 2:30 by the time I tore my numbered ticket off at the DMV. I didn't have to check the monitor to know I was going to be in line for a long time. The place was packed. I found a clerk who pulled a commercial driving manual out from behind the counter, and started reading. Skimming is more like it, but with laser focus. I had to pass the test on the first try. (I've got this!)

On the drive to the DMV, I called Judy Manella, the Kids 'R' Kids franchise owner I mentioned previously. Judy always seemed to have a solution. She gave me the name of a certified CDL instructor who might be able to help me. Tim taught truck drivers during the week and didn't mind picking up a few extra bucks on the weekends. Tim was my best and only shot if I wanted to be driving on Monday.

I was in luck. He answered his cell phone and said he could meet me on Saturday—as long as I had the DMV paper saying I was eligible for a learner's permit. He could train me and issue a permit by Sunday. The rest was up to me. (I've got this!)

By the time my number flashed, it was after 4 p.m. and the clerk said it was too late to take the CDL test; they required no less than one hour. I explained my plight, with emphasis, and promised I'd be fast. He obliged with grace. I passed and he smiled as he handed me the signed temporary permit. I thanked him, smiled back, and snatched it out of his hand. One down. The next hurdle would come tomorrow.

Alex had agreed to ride with me in the bus to the driving center to meet Tim. It was my first time behind the wheel, and I confess, it was pretty thrilling! It was a big bus, designed for 54 passengers, and brand spanking new. The engine purred as we went down the expressway. (Whoa! I've really got this!)

Tim was a swell guy and put me right at ease. After a few hours of practice, emergency drills, and bus mechanics, I had my legal temporary CDL in hand to go with the big smile on my face. I drove the bus back to Kids 'R' Kids with my plan in motion to do a practice run of the entire route on Sunday. Done and done.

On Monday morning, amid much giggling, clapping, and cheering from the children, staff, and even several parents, I drove the first of many bus runs that fall. It was an experience I still cherish because I got to know the students and school partners in ways I would never have if I had not been willing to step into that Unplanned Leadership role.

In the fall of 1998 we served two elementary schools. By 2012, we had three buses, three locations, and served eleven schools for before- and after-school care. There were many days over the course of those years when I drove the bus. Sometimes it was for a field trip I wanted to experience with the children, and some days I just wanted to get out of the office and connect with the kids and the team. Every time I did, I felt proud, re-charged, and happy that I was the kind of boss who was willing and able to drive the bus.

Think about the most critical positions in your franchise. What if that person quit with no notice or had a sudden and serious illness? If it's a lead cook, trainer, graphic designer, or lead cashier, could you jump in? The television show "Undercover Boss" does a great service by showing us how difficult it is to work in many of the positions we take for granted. You'll meet one of them in **Chapter 13: If You Build It, They Will Come ...** which focuses on being competitive. There are many potential Unplanned Leadership scenarios waiting to happen in every franchise. Imagine the leadership capital you would build by volunteering to cover for one of those positions, and picture yourself saying, "I've got this!"

UNPLANNED LEADERSHIP EXERCISE

List three to five areas where think your business is most vulnerable.

_____

_____

_____

_____

_____

Pick the top two that are most likely to happen and describe the impact if it happened.

_____

_____

Develop a potential leadership strategy to proactively address each one. I recommend outlining a few simple steps that you can later define and refine.

Strategy #1:

_____

_____

_____

_____

_____

Strategy #2

_____

_____

_____

_____

_____

Responsive Leadership

If Unplanned Leadership is what strong Leaders do *as* something *happens*, Responsive Leadership is what happens in the *aftermath* of something that *has happened*. As an owner, you have the opportunity to act in response to things that happen every single day. Choosing what to respond to is a daily opportunity to display leadership. Not responding to something minor is a form of leadership, too, because you are not micromanaging and you expect accountability. Conversely, not responding to something significant that occurred is an unrealized Responsive Leadership opportunity and over time can create deep rifts in your organization, leading to turnover and soon, decreased revenue. Many owners practice this type of non-leadership hoping a situation will improve. Not Rob Krecak, the uBreakiFix franchisee you met in the beginning of this chapter.

When I interviewed Rob, I didn't ask him specifically why he started incorporating his business and life principles into his new hire process, probably because I was so drawn in by his motivational coaching philosophy. (Hypothetically, let's assume that it was because he wanted to hire the highest-quality employees possible in response to having some less-than-stellar hires in the past.) Rob chose Responsive Leadership by imprinting his personal values throughout the franchise culture, starting with the interview process.

Rob created a manifesto of sorts that he uses to guide the interview in a way that shows who is the best fit and most desires being "the best version of yourself personally and professionally." If they don't convince Rob, they don't make the cut. His candid and selective hiring Responsive Leadership strategy has no doubt addressed his "hypothetical" goal and produced many like-minded employees who are grateful for the opportunity to be led and mentored by him.

On a weekly basis, Responsive Leaders are tuned into the rhythm of their business and recognize the early warning signs of a downward shift in morale. A Responsive Leader knows a few conversations and a slight increase in engagement are all that are needed to zero in on the origin of the dip in morale and then takes steps to address it. When cash flow unexpectedly slows down, a Responsive Leader is able to scale back payroll ever so gently without drama or hardship while also very slightly turning up the marketing program to ease the business back to where it needs to be.

Here are three examples from my personal experience. They aren't pretty, but I'll bet you will relate.

- **Letting good people go.** One of my favorite directors, Julie, had proven herself to be extremely hard-working, bright, and sufficiently "tough enough" to manage almost 50 employees when she asked about hiring her sister for a teaching position. I didn't have a formal policy to address this and said, "Sure, let's interview her" and then, "Sure, let's hire her." The sister also proved herself to be a hard worker and was well-liked by the children and parents—*when she was there*. The problem was, she was missing a lot of work. The reasons were personal and I was aware and sympathetic, but still, I was running a business and absenteeism was well-documented throughout the center. Excessive absenteeism was not permitted.

    I was not the only one who had noticed. By the time I seriously discussed my concern with Julie, the staff had started rumbling about favoritism towards her sister. It was no wonder. Julie was a rock-solid director and ran a tight ship. She frequently denied requests for time off if the coverage was not available or requests were excessive. She did not apply the same standards to her sister and it was obvious. Within months, Julie lost the respect of the staff and employee morale was starting to plunge because I was letting this continue. In fact, the feedback about Julie's management that I had received during the annual employee survey discussed in **Chapter 3: Show Employees You Care (and Make It Count!)** confirmed how upset the other employees were. So, by the time I insisted that it was time to terminate her sister, my inner voice was shouting, "Start looking for Julie's replacement!"

There was another issue with this director—one that was not public knowledge and was not sitting well with me. It seemed ever since she had gotten married and now had health insurance through her husband's company, she had lost sight of the importance of the 90-day benefits review and we were in danger of not having enough participants to maintain our rates, putting our benefits package in jeopardy. Being able to offer benefits was part of my professional mission and a competitive (recruiting) advantage. This was not acceptable. I had already taken back this part of her job function when I asked her to terminate her sister.

With this knowledge, you might wonder why I was hesitant. Here's why: Julie was several months pregnant and she represented a minority demographic. For those reasons and because I cared about her well-being, I consulted the employment attorney, whom I kept on retainer, before letting her go. I missed her; however, before long the ship had been righted and it was business as usual with high morale intact. The best part of this story and the lesson I learned was that I distinctly noticed an added measure of leadership respect and loyalty from my staff, who knew I'd made a difficult decision.

- **When it's time for a big hire.** It's hard to know when it's time to add that first or next key person. It's not something they cover at franchise training, especially if you are ambitiously expanding. If I was feeling a little bored before the Enrichment Center expansion, then after it was up and running I was wondering why I hadn't enjoyed that time more. I was now completely swamped and (another confession) feeling overwhelmed even though the cash flow was very good. I didn't like my business much that year—my first "red flag." And I wasn't the only one. Employee morale was suffering. My staff didn't like seeing me so busy and stressed, and they missed, as I did, the informal one-on-one talks I used to have time for. I wondered what else might be suffering in my business and what else I was missing that might be lurking. I soon found out. All I knew for sure was that I was at my upper limit and it was time to take the next big step and hire a general manager.

The primary issue was that this was uncharted water. This was not a position that other centers had and so, after consulting my franchisor for advice, I made sure I was bringing in enough cash flow. I wanted someone strong and experienced, and that takes a good salary. I decided to think about it for a few more days when Karen walked in at the end of an evening to pick up her boys. Karen was one of my favorite clients. She had been at the center for many years, and I always tried to make time to talk to her whenever I could. I knew she worked hard and that she managed workers compensation and loss management for a large industrial employer. What I didn't know, until that moment, was that she was also ready for a change.

I trusted her. We had known each other for years and our boys were friends. After I somewhat casually revealed my frustration to her, she surprised me by saying that perhaps she could help. We gave each other the "Oh my gosh, this is crazy good!" look and knew instantly it was a great match. I could hire someone I trusted, and she could be closer to home and spend more time with her boys by her side at work.

With Karen at the helm, I was able to enjoy the work and the people who dedicated their work life to what we were doing, *together*. There was now time for spontaneous moments in the classroom and casual conversations with staff and parents. Time that I had to forego when I insisted on doing it all myself. I do not know what would have happened had I not realized it was time to proactively respond to the growing needs of a growing business. I'm only glad I had a leadership style that kept me from finding out. My guess is that it would not have been very pretty and certainly not *nearly* as much fun.

- **It's still broken until you (really) fix it.** When we left the section on Unplanned Leadership, I was waxing about the wonderful synergies of having stepped in to drive the bus while I hired a full-time key person to replace Alex. It was, indeed, an excellent experience; however, there was more. Much more. The work to make sure this did not happen again had just begun. Enter "Miss Christy—Responsive Leader."

Step one was to hire Alex's replacement. Once that was done, the real work started. I laid out a plan that centered on having in-house substitute drivers. In other words, simple cross-training. In this case, however, it wasn't so simple. Most infant, toddler, and preschool teachers are female. Most ladies don't have "Learning to drive a bus" on their list of career goals and certainly not on their bucket list, so I had to get creative. I put together a program I hoped might be enticing enough to interest a few brave souls and started recruiting.

The program included an introductory bus run to see what they were getting into, an immediate fifty-cents-an-hour raise upon completion of the exam, a $150 bonus when the CDL was in hand, and a quarterly team lunch meeting. I saved the best for last: You will be out of the classroom when you are driving the bus!

Several people signed up and the program was launched. Each year, depending on the needs of the organization, I'd have a new class. The Bus Team ended up being an integral part of the business as we launched ahead on an aggressive growth trajectory adding new schools each year. They worked well together as a team and solved many problems before I even knew they existed. I stayed in lead position of the team and never gave up my CDL because I, too, liked to get out of the building and hear that sweet diesel engine purr. Remembering the childrens' laughter and excitement on pickup runs still warms my heart.

When something happens, the Responsive Leader analyzes the situation, formulates an improvement plan, and then executes. Early and regular communication and transparency are vital to building the deep loyalty and commitment that follows a Responsive Leader. The Responsive Leader's staff and clients know the organization is under the watch of a very capable and committed owner who does not shy away from problems and organizational challenges.

What does the Responsible Leader do to inspire such high praise and loyalty? The answer lies in one simple phrase: The Responsive Leader A-C-T-S. If you have work to do in this area, take heart; you are in the majority. Responsive Leadership is a skill-set that can developed, and it is never too late to start.

RESPONSIVE LEADERSHIP EXERCISE

Brainstorm three to five areas where you need to lead proactively to better protect and strengthen your business.

1. _____
2. _____
3. _____
4. _____
5. _____

Pick two that you are ready to commit to and describe what the impact would be on your business.

1. _____
2. _____

Develop a potential leadership strategy to proactively address each one. I recommend outlining a few simple steps that you can later define and refine.

Strategy #1:

_____

_____

_____

_____

_____

Strategy #2

_____

_____

_____

_____

_____

Planned Leadership

Planned Leadership demonstrates to your stakeholders that you are here to stay and you are ready to Go Big.

Going Big means your actions get noticed. You strategically choose your target stakeholder, your methods, and the amount of money and time you are going to commit to this year. You control the variables, the plan, and the execution. Going Big with Planned Leadership creates a tremendous amount of security and stability in your business and workplace because your actions show you have the health and growth of the organization at the top of your mind.

You met Ali Geiger, a very successful Dream Vacations, World Travel Holdings franchisee, in **Chapter 3: Show Employees You Care (and Make It Count!)** when we focused on building employee loyalty. She showed she is a strategic leader when she shared this during our interview:

> "I started a monthly newsletter for my clients that they really love, and I have a link on my website and my Facebook page that makes it easy for anyone to access and share. I talked about it at conference with other owners who liked it, and corporate allowed me to make it available to other franchisees. I charge an annual subscription fee, paid by the owners, and they customize it to fit their market and clients."

Way to go, Ali. Her Go Big Planned Leadership touches her clients, associates, and franchisor, and it clearly has the potential to draw in new clients through social media sharing. It shows how Planned Leadership puts you in control of your business, your future, and your success *this year.* It is your opportunity to show vision and commitment in a way that clearly defines who you are. *You are a successful, forward-thinking franchisee who cares about your business, your clients, your staff, and your community.*

Planned Leadership is such a significant success differentiator that I have devoted an entire chapter to it, and we will dive into it next. You'll learn more about how to Go Big as you continue to build the Strategic Leadership Pillar in the following chapter.

In this chapter, you learned how Strategic Leadership helps you protect your business because you respond appropriately when opportunities and challenges are presented. Your business runs more smoothly and grows faster when you add Planned Leadership. You will soon be in a much better position to lead exactly where you want to go with this final leadership strategy. Are you ready to Go Big?

CHAPTER 7

Who Are You Leading This Year?

Central Florida is a hotbed for competitors, and it can be a big challenge to retain good team members. To build loyalty and to be successful, you have to be involved shoulder to shoulder with the team, making sure you give them the heart and hustle of the organization. It's only done right if the entire team does it right. That means you might be making sandwiches at lunchtime or working behind the register.

Scott Anthony

Orlando, Florida
Firehouse Subs franchisee since 2002
Co-owner of 12 Firehouse Subs restaurants in Central Florida
with plans to develop others in Wisconsin

As much as you want to or think you can, you cannot lead everyone equally and purposefully every year and expect to see positive outcomes in every area. It's simply too big a job, and trying to do that leads to stress, burnout, and serious health or family issues. Early on I tried, and it took being stopped for suspicion of driving under the influence to stop me from trying to lead everyone all the time. The stress had led to unhealthy choices, and that was my wake-up call. Instead of casting a huge leadership net that likely has plenty of holes, be the type of leader your staff needs and craves, and the leader your business requires—*this* year.

Planned Leadership

Every franchisee has three stakeholder groups that will require an annual leadership plan: clients, staff, and community. The question is, based on your planned revenue growth number, who specifically within those three groups can have the highest impact on your revenue? The answer to that question is where you will focus your Planned Leadership resources this year. And not just focus— you are going to Go Big! Going Big is what will make a real difference because people will notice what you do. It's how strong leaders use their leadership capital to strengthen, protect, and grow their businesses. And it all starts with one question: *Who, specifically, are you going to lead this year?*

The first answer to that question should be *yourself.*

Go Big Plan: Personal Leadership

Every year, I made sure I had a planning meeting that included a heart-to-heart with myself in order review my leadership shortcomings and goals for the year. The objective was to identify what stood in the way of my ability *this year* to have a successful Go Big Leadership Plan. Because it was a private meeting, I had no excuse to be anything but brutally frank. Here's an example of my private meeting the year my ex-husband and son's father passed away suddenly, and I turned 50:

Personal Health Management

I knew I was exhausted that year but had not addressed it. I was still trying to be all things to everyone and when I tried to drive home after consuming too many Pinot Grigios during a girls' night out birthday celebration with the old school gang. I was stressed out and worn out but went anyway. The officer who stopped me didn't care that it was my birthday. I'm glad he didn't. It was the wake-up call I needed, and I thanked God it didn't turn out worse and that I could afford a good attorney.

Other than being totally embarrassed and struggling to keep the whole incident a secret, nothing really had changed. At least not at first. I was still a full-time single mom and still running out the door from work every afternoon to pick up the kiddo and still not as fully present as I wanted to be at work or at home. But I knew it wasn't working anymore. My son's needs had changed and we were both mourning his Dad. It was time to get serious about restructuring my afternoon and evening commitments, and to get some help at home.

I hired a college student to help me with Mom duties in the afternoon. She was a lifesaver. When my son got older, I kept her on as a personal assistant to help with grocery shopping and other errands, and then hired a "manny" who took Roland to the gym and Boy Scouts.

For a couple hundred dollars a week, I was able to focus on my business during the high-impact afternoons and I knew my son was well cared for and was thrilled to have a male influence in his life. I had food in my house, gifts were sent on time, and I was able enjoy my weekends now that I wasn't spending them running errands. My stress level decreased exponentially when I slowed down, and I added regular yoga classes to my schedule.

I share this personal story to show you what I mean by having a serious heart-to-heart with yourself once a year. My hope is that my story might prevent you from one of the many real-life impacts of having too much "everything" in your life. Over your time as an owner, it's likely you will experience one of the leading stressors in life, including death of a loved one, divorce, or health issues. If my story speaks to you in any way and you have not already made changes to address what you need to, your private meeting is the time to do it. No excuses and *no shame*.

Professional Goal Setting

Here are some other things that could be keeping you from Going Big with Planned Leadership this year.

- **Fear of failure**: From making a capital investment to moving your office out of the spare bedroom and into a leased space, is fear keeping you from taking action?

- **Micromanaging:** Do you feel the need to manage the details of everything on your weekly and monthly task list? Could that be thwarting your efforts to get out into the community?
- **Outside commitments:** Have community commitments crept into your week to the point you are not as focused and effective? Are you using those commitments as a way, an excuse even, to not fully engage with your management team or your clients or to plan for the upcoming year?
- **Avoidance and denial:** Are you avoiding a plan to deal with a new competitor? Has revenue slowed down and you can't find the time to figure out why? Are you not fully up to speed on a new software or service and avoid learning about it?

Noted business writer and author of *Swim with the Sharks Without Getting Eaten Alive*, Harvey Mackay, writes that "To become the best leader you can be, you must take advantage of every opportunity to learn and improve." He also says leaders "must set an example for their employees. If they have stopped learning and growing, they will be hard pressed to inspire their subordinates to do so, no matter how much they may pretend to encourage it." I made it a practice to have one of my personal plans include some type of career development. Examples of my Go Big Personal Leadership plans included joining monthly Directors Association lunch-and-learn meetings and earning a Director Credential certification.

I learned the hard way that you have to strategically lead yourself before you can lead your clients, staff, and community. It took a long time before I really understood how important it was to be truly comprehensive about this plan. Make the commitment to refine your personal leadership objectives and activities for this year so you can drive other programs in a more relaxed state of mind from your place at the top. Take a few minutes now to complete the following exercise and address your weak link:

PERSONAL LEADERSHIP EXERCISE

What is keeping you from being a Strategic Leader?

Personal:

_____

_____

_____

Professional:

_____

_____

_____

List two possible solutions for each area you identified.

Personal:

1. _____

2. _____

Professional:

_____

_____

Identify one solution from each category that you could implement within 90 days and write a basic action plan of three to five steps for each one. Don't think too long or hard about this; you will refine it at a later time.

Personal Action Plan:

1. _____

2. _____

3. _____

Professional Action Plan:

1. _____

2. _____

3. _____

Go Big Plan: Client Leadership

When it comes to Client Leadership, you want to focus on a well-developed and well-planned strategy that will appeal to your best (Sweet Spot) clients and attract new ones and others who will add profitable revenue to your bottom line this year. Remember, it wouldn't be a Go Big Leadership strategy if it were easy. This is yours to lead.

Here's an example to help explain this:

One of my Sweet Spot Client profiles was parents who had two or more children. As a working mother with one child, I was always in awe of how these families juggled the many challenges and stressors associated with managing a household, scheduling activities, working full-time, and (not least!) having a successful marriage. One year, based on questions asked on a survey, I decided that the Go Big Leadership plan I would do that year was to organize a series of evening parent workshops with topics to be determined by clients. (I had attended something similar at my son's previous preschool and found it to be very helpful). No shame in borrowing a good idea, and as far as I knew, none of my competitors had done anything like this. *Even better.*

With input, I determined the best night of the week and relevant topics. I found professionals who were willing to facilitate a topic without charging a fee. I promoted the workshops externally at pediatrician and dental offices, family restaurants, and other places working parents went. I was able to Go Big—leading existing clients and attracting new potential clients because it was planned in advance and was well-thought-out. Our staff provided childcare and enjoyed the additional pay. We served a light meal. The parents enjoyed it and were very complementary, and we gained several new clients.

I decided not to offer it the following year. Upon reflection, I determined that although the synergies were there for building deeper loyalty for clients and staff members, the events were not as successful as I needed them to be in order to justify my leadership time and the franchise's resources.

Other Go Big examples could be new signage, a new way of communication with your clients such as starting a texting service or e-newsletter, or adding an annual client event such as a golf tournament or open house.

Go Big Client Leadership Exercise

Brainstorm three to five ways you could demonstrate leadership to your clients.

1. _____
2. _____
3. _____
4. _____
5. _____

Identify which of these would be most likely to also attract new Sweet Spot Clients. Circle it.

Pick one and outline a basic three- to five-step plan that you would be willing and able to do this year.

1. _____
2. _____
3. _____
4. _____
5. _____

Go Big Plan: Employee Leadership

A Go Big Plan for Employee Leadership addresses a specific area of your staffing that will noticeably and directly impact your franchise this year. You may want to begin by looking back on the past year before tackling this one unless you know absolutely what you need to do this year. Payroll reports revealed a lot, including significant events I had forgotten about or completely *blocked out*. I used human resources firm ADP's system for many years and found the data and easy formatting to be invaluable. With your notepad ready, start mining for trends and high-impact or surprising occurrences.

Typical questions to get started include: Are your tenured employees carrying their weight or do they need retraining or motivation? Is your staff being reviewed consistently and fairly? Do you have a formalized career development plan to attract and retain good employees who may want to grow with you? Are your rates of pay in good order, and would they score well if they were tested for fairness? Is your rate of pay too low? Have you used an employee survey to get feedback and gauge satisfaction?

You can't tackle them all in one year, but you may see a pattern that, with the right Go Big Plan, can address many simultaneously and synergistically. For example, if your turnover rate is high and you have determined it's related to the poor quality of candidates, your Go Big Plan for employees would be to develop a resource and the means to draw in a better pool of applicants, and perhaps review and change your interview process.

Here's what I did two years back-to-back when I needed to Go Big:

Year One – Frustrated I didn't have enough certified instructors to meet my upcoming state accreditation requirement, I made a plan to actively recruit newly certified Child Development Associates (CDAs) from the local educational institutions. It worked. We added enough CDAs to renew our accreditation, but my planning review the following year showed that new hires who had a commute didn't stick around long.

Year Two – Frustrated the CDAs I hired didn't last long, I chose to Go Big by offering the training and certification on-site for existing non-CDA staff. Participants received one raise when they enrolled and another one with completion, and I covered the tuition cost. Turnover decreased, and because literally the entire staff was credentialed, I later used it as a competitive advantage. I'll come back to how this synergistic surprise was put to good use in the Money Metrics – Pillar 3 section.

Here are a few Go Big strategies I implemented for employee leadership that should help you develop yours:

- Added department-specific quarterly training to build knowledge and teamwork
- Introduced career book club meetings to enhance career development and team-building
- Realigned to create new supervisor positions to improve communication and add career opportunities

- Added benefits (one year) and paid time off (another year) to address turnover and increase loyalty
- Implemented a merit and demerit system

GO BIG EMPLOYEE LEADERSHIP EXERCISE

List three to five of the biggest challenges you experience with your employees.

1. _____
2. _____
3. _____
4. _____
5. _____

What, if anything, do they have in common? Regroup them if applicable.

_____
_____
_____
_____
_____

Circle the challenge that, if eliminated, would have the biggest potential to change your business for the good.

Brainstorm three Go Big ideas (to be developed later) that, if done right, would have the depth and scope to substantially improve or eliminate this problem.

1. _____
2. _____
3. _____

Go Big Plan: Community Leadership

As with clients and employees, the choice of who to lead is wide open, so it's important to take your time reviewing the options and the return on investment

(ROI) of time and energy before making any commitments. As with developing Layers of Community Loyalty, being extremely selective cannot be overstated here. Remember, we are being strategic because you are (only!) one person who needs to display leadership to your staff, your clients, and your community—*not* change the world.

If you have already developed some Layers of Community Loyalty, you may be halfway there. You have no doubt learned a great deal about what you *do not* want to do, and that's extremely valuable. Now let's look at two types of strategic community leadership: professional associations and social causes.

Professional Associations

- **Local:** Professional associations are almost always very welcoming to people who want to get involved, even as a basic member. There are many benefits of membership, including networking opportunities with local business owners and prospects and as a resource for finding quality employees. If your franchise has one or two up-and-coming managers or supervisors, association memberships can provide career development opportunities. They benefit professionally when you invite them to join you for a lunch-and-learn meeting or after-hours networking. The right association has the potential to address Employee Loyalty and Employee Leadership as well as Community Loyalty and Community Leadership. That's a subtle but powerful Go Big synergy bonus.

- **Industry:** Since becoming a member of the International Franchise Association (IFA), I've been impressed by the high quality of professionals who volunteer. From Melanie Bergeron, CEO of Two Men and a Truck in 2015, to Aziz Hashim, Managing Partner of NRD Capital in 2016, and now Shelly Sun of BrightStar Care, all three of these individuals gave their time to serve as Chair. Clearly, this uber-high level of commitment is not for everyone. But think about your specific franchise segment and how your involvement with a professional association that aligns with your goals and values can show you're a leader who is committed to your field. Then think about how the repeated exposure to your brand might yield trickle-down revenue and growth benefits.

I used this type of Go Big Leadership to focus on my franchise segment as a board member of the local public television station and the Community Coordinated Care for Children, which distributes state funds to low-income working parents. I found both experiences to be extremely rewarding and clients and prospects often commented on the plaques hanging in the lobby. Each position required no more than four hours a month.

Social Causes

Buying local and doing business with companies that are aligned with and contribute to a social cause are two trends that are not going away anytime soon. It's critical you position your franchise very purposefully and strategically in order to win the favor of the rapidly growing number of discerning local socially conscious consumers. Even if your target clients include businesses rather than consumers—as do many printing, tax, and signage franchises, many of your clients are concerned with social causes and may choose a competitor that actively demonstrates a social cause alignment.

The "Age of Accountability" is here and no one cares about this more than consumers and managers in the Millennial generation, born roughly between the early 1980s and early 2000s. I spend hours each week teaching this demographic business courses, and they are very serious about this topic. Again, I strongly recommend doing very thoughtful research and planning before making a commitment. In other words, be strategic.

Many franchisors have taken the lead on this. If yours has, then say thank you and make sure you're engaged in the success of the program by participating and sharing what you're doing on social media and with your clients. As a leader, this is how you display to your community that you are local, more than just a chain and that you care about much more than simply making money. Brainstorm how you can organize a community event to call attention to the cause. Let your employees get involved before you get too far into the planning stages. Connecting with your local community can be personally rewarding and motivational for everyone involved. Use that.

If your franchisor has not designated a specific cause, develop your own. Look for one that aligns with your core service or products and the values of your company and your stakeholders. Make phone calls, send emails, and meet with organizations before making a decision or commitment. They should be responsive and able to give you some ideas about what would be most beneficial. Only then you can determine whether the organization would be a good match.

Gone are the days when writing a check passes as "doing good." If they only want your money, you should not consider them viable for your Go Big Leadership Plan. You want your efforts to be meaningful which means having a participative relationship that will create synergies, like teamwork, while you do good things *together*. Being recognized as a local small business owner who cares will not be lost on your staff and your clients. They will respect your leadership contribution and will show it with increased loyalty and referrals.

Your professional fulfillment and positive attitude will be infectious, and your community goodwill will increase each year as you continue to lead in such an impactful way. Remember Eddie Titen and BBQ To The Rescue from **Chapter 4: Connect with Your Community**? *That's* what I'm talking about. If you don't happen to have a really cool tricked-out truck to deliver delicious free food, start thinking and figure out what you *do* have. Be strategic and they will come.

The Wow Factor Plus You

It is imperative all of your Go Big Leadership plans pass the "wow" test. When you reveal your employee plan to your managers and staff, and your client plan in your newsletter, you want the intended target to say, "Wow! This is going to be great!" If that doesn't happen, then it probably isn't big enough. In other words, make it count. Make it matter in the lives of the people you're targeting with your plan.

Making it count includes making sure your Go Big plans reflect your values and vision for your business. Making this challenging choice each year and announcing it publicly shows your community of stakeholders that you intend to stay on top of your business. That's the mark you want to hit. When your plan reflects who you are, you are much more likely to maintain the passion and commitment it takes to see it through. That's hitting the Go Big bulls-eye.

How and when you communicate your Go Big plans will greatly impact the success of your strategy. The next chapter will help ensure your plans are successful and your Strategic Leadership messages are received—every time.

CHAPTER 8

Communication:
The Ultimate Differentiator

I use Facebook on a regular basis to share ideas to build our value and engage the team across 12 states because it's easy for everyone to access and it appeals to the younger generations. I've turned to videos for personal training and membership training. We had a manual, but the videos eliminated that and the motivation and care required to be successful come through much better now. I still talk to everyone on the floor, and everyone has my cell phone number. Anybody can shoot me a text and we'll role play together on the phone if their metric is off.

Jeff O'Mara

Manilla, Indiana
Anytime Fitness franchisee since 2007
Multi-club owner in Indiana, Ohio, Tennessee, and Georgia
Regional Franchise Advisory Council representative

My book development editor, Juli Baldwin, suggested I put this chapter earlier in the book. Juli correctly recognized that virtually everything about building the 4 Pillars is dependent on communication. Instead, I put communication in the Leadership pillar because it's your leadership that drives the communication that pushes your business forward and keeps your business relevant. When you are in control of your business, your communication reflects that. This falls squarely on your shoulders, and you need to get this right.

In order to move your business from where it is today to the next level and then to the top tier in your system, you'll need a solid communication process. Jeff figured that out long before he branched out to four states and relies heavily on it today to manage fourteen gyms. Without a process to communicate your programs and plans and engage consistently with your team and your clients, your results may be only half of what you want and need to attain your revenue goals this year. Half of the people will get the messages, and half of them will not. Half is not enough to get you where you want to be.

Your communication process should not be complicated, just rock solid. Your objective is to identify the right time and the right modes, or ways, to communicate your programs for each of the target stakeholders and then to *be consistent*. Know in advance that communication is challenging because of the discipline and creativity required, but it gets easier the more you practice. Jeff didn't say so, but I'll bet he used a lot of things that didn't work before he settled on his process. He stuck with it—and it clearly pays dividends now.

Of course, we are going to break this down strategically.

The Wrong Way to Communicate

You are not alone if you find yourself often frustrated when your communication raises more questions than it answers. John T. Hewitt, founder of Liberty Tax Service, says this in his 2016 book *iCompete: How My Extraordinary Strategy for Winning Can Be Yours:* "When it comes to communication, no one gets it right." I agree with John. It's hard to hit the bulls-eye with communication. You have many communication hurdles to consider. With three major stakeholder groups relying on you and the multiple communication options available and used today, it's important to regularly evaluate your effectiveness and be willing to adapt as your environment changes. I learned this the hard way (of course!) the first time I had a price increase.

In the early childhood education field, most franchisees are allowed to set their own prices. It's up to franchisees to assess the local market and increase, or decrease prices to reflect their positioning as conditions change. After having been open for two years, I decided it was time to raise my prices. I published the new tuition rates worksheet reflecting my eight percent to ten percent increase with an effective date of January 1 and asked the teachers to put the notice with a letter from me attached in each child's take-home file in early December. Plenty of notice and simple enough, right? Wrong, wrong, and wrong. My clients were furious. Most were not aware of the increase until they went to pay in January and were told they owed additional money. Happy bleeping New Year to me. I wanted to hide behind the counter. It was ugly.

From that experience, I learned multiple valuable lessons on how *not* to communicate and determined I would work hard to get it right. And not just for the touchy stuff, like price increases or cutting back staff hours, but for routine things as well. I learned that communication, like so many other aspects of your business, has to be strategic so it consistently hits the target, if not the center, in the right way *every* time. I became obsessed with this, and that obsession served me well going forward.

Hedge Your Bet: Run the Table with Different Modes

I found early on that the best approach for my business was to not rely on any single method but to use several in order to ensure the intended receiver would, in fact, get the message. I'll bet that's true for your business as well. There are two very good reasons you should use multiple communication modes for a single message.

First, people take in information differently, and it's your job to find at least one for everyone. If your clients and staff range from Millennials to Baby Boomers, you have a lot of modes to cover when you announce a new promotion, a schedule change or price increase. And cover them you must. Protecting your business depends on successful communication.

The second reason you should hedge your bet with multiple modes is what we've learned from marketing experts: that it is better to hear something more than once in order to make it "stick." This is not the time to be shy or overly polite. Get it out there. The good and the bad. With the price increase, my first mistake was to assume everyone would take home the tuition rate sheet. They did not. My second mistake was to assume they would read it. Hardly anyone did. I also should have sent it in an email, posted it in plain view, and added it to the daily check-in computer announcements for at least 10 days. I should have interspersed the aforementioned communications over a full month leading up to the price increase instead of making one announcement, with one mode thirty days in advance.

My excuse? I was young, naïve, and inexperienced. I was also scared. Although my research was fact-based and I needed to raise prices, my instincts were also right. The jump was too big. Subconsciously, and honestly, it may have been my fear of the client backlash that prevented me from being more forthright with the notification. Regardless, not getting the message out correctly made it much, much worse. I learned a lot from that dreadful experience.

Going forward, there was a checklist or process for all important communications. Stress was decreased at the front desk, and the future annual two percent to three percent price increases generated little or no pushback from clients. The depth and breadth of the communication made all the difference.

Look for Signs, Then Ask Questions

I usually knew when I wasn't communicating deeply enough or wasn't going wide enough, and you will, too. If new inquiries have fallen off, you may need to communicate your referral program more consistently or try a different mode to deliver the message. If applications for employment are barely trickling in, try announcing during your next networking or professional gathering that "At (pet related franchise), we are always looking for good employees who love (animals *and* people)." And then hand out a small promotional piece to remind them and thank them in advance. Spot-check with employees ("What did you think about the such-and-such change that was announced?") to see if they read your Facebook post or email. Also spot-check with clients ("Do you think our new delivery service will be something that will benefit you soon?") to see if they know about your promotion. Ask a question in your next survey that relates to communication.

Be tenacious. You need to know what is working and what is preferred. Your stakeholders will respect that you asked *and* you will get valuable information that will save you frustration and time.

COMMUNICATION EXERCISE

Current: List the three primary ways and the frequency with which you communicate to your three stakeholder groups. Describe, where applicable, how each mode applies to each group. Consider dropping or changing any modes that seem outdated or are ineffective.

Future: Add two new modes with approximate start dates and stakeholder targets to balance your communication plan for the coming year.

Communication Method	Clients	Staff	Community
Current			
Current			
Current			
Future			
Future			

Make It Engaging

Like Jeff O'Mara, keep communication fresh by trying new things. In his quote he basically said that he is making manuals obsolete by filming his own Anytime Fitness training videos. Jeff is uber-engaging and authentic. I watched some of his videos and he is smart to use his strength (pun intended) to enhance staff training. Having a lighthearted message in between the serious stuff is great, too. At Kids 'R' Kids, Tracy Musgrave, the general manager you'll meet in

Chapter 16: Meetings Aren't Sexy, but Accountability Is, was a master at social media and all things creative. Because we had permission to film and photograph the children for noncommercial purposes, she would occasionally shoot a short video about what we did that week as she walked around from class to class. She would then email a link to our clients. Some clients posted these links on their own Facebook page and shared it with grandparents all over the country. They also shared it at the office. *Score.*

For the scavenger hunts and trivia contests I referenced earlier, we hid the clues and listed the questions in between the center business news within the newsletter, which usually ensured it got read. I didn't hesitate to sign up when a company that was referred by the corporate office called about having seasonal messages when people were placed on telephone hold. Six times a year I could change the music and the message. I usually chose two messages that informed about our services, two that were humorous parenting tips, and two that were seasonal.

Today I spend a fair amount of time on social media. I never did as a franchise owner. I now know I should have. Lucky for me, I had Tracy, who made sure we had a presence. Many franchisors, including many represented in this book, do an incredible job of making the social media communications fun and engaging, and they have the ability to make a fervent brand ambassador out of the most mild-mannered consumer. If your franchisor has set the tone for this, jump on board and use that communication. Match it to your location and territory through your own social media. Proceed with caution at first. Some franchisors have strict rules of engagement for social media.

If you are not currently on several franchisors' email lists, choose a few brands you know and sign up. You might get some great ideas for your franchise and will be in a much better position to understand how your own franchisor has positioned your brand.

Own It—Or It Will Own You

That subconscious hesitation to be fully transparent and forthcoming was something I battled, especially in the beginning. I learned, over time, that sharing information, especially the tough things, was a quick path to building trust. I did not withhold important information from my clients or staff, but I did try to give the information in the right quantity and on a need-to-know basis.

I think that approach works well for most franchises and most segments. When it came to matters relating to safety, I usually concluded just about everybody needed to know. Think about a few of the worst things that could happen in your business as you read through these two examples of owning up and going wide with communications.

Remember the story about Stingray Boy? That's the little boy who was literally wandering the neighborhood when he should have been at my center. I could have chosen to keep that quiet. It was pretty ugly. Good thing I didn't. As you know, we had a visit by the local news crew a couple of weeks later, which would have blown the lid off my little secret and blown my credibility to shreds. What I chose to do instead was to put it "out there." All of it. The facts of what happened were explained in a memo that was sent home and emailed to all parents. In addition to the facts, our new policy was included and the memo stated that we expected route delays as we acclimated to the new policy. By the time the news crew showed up, my clients and staff were fairly nonplussed about the whole thing. The disappointed reporter heard phrases like, "Yes, of course we are aware!" and "Yes, the owner handled this."

Remember a few years ago, when the MERS virus (Middle East Respiratory Syndrome) had everyone scared to death? Healthcare franchisors and children's service franchises were on high alert and so were we. Then it happened. A child who attended our school was suspected of having this potentially life-threatening respiratory virus.

We posted the appropriate notice, as required by the Florida Department of Children and Families and in accordance with our franchise agreement. When I say posted, I mean it was on every single classroom door. For days I reassured people that, according to the child's doctor, it was in all likelihood not MERS but their child's safety was our first concern and we always err on the side of caution. I wrote a brief memo that went out in multiple modes to all families and staff members explaining our policy and what we were doing.

The posted signs stayed up even as the child was cleared by the doctor to return to school. The sigh of relief was audible. That weekend, I was hosting a party for the staff in the center gym. On Sunday, probably procrastinating my office work, I wandered around the building and ripped down the MERS signs off the classroom doors. On Monday, right about pickup time, the local news crew showed up at the front door with cameras pointed, asking about the MERS case at the school. The timing was all wrong. The case had been cleared the prior week. Had they been extremely busy at the TV station the week before, or had a staff member brought a guest to the party who saw the signs and tipped off the station?

Again, the clients were the heroes because they calmly responded to the reporters' probing questions in defense of "our" school. "No, we were not scared for our children" and "We knew the owner was on top of it." I could not have said it better myself. Another disappointed reporter left with another non-story. *Next!*

When you are consistent and upfront with your communication, your staff and clients are secure in the knowledge that you are a trustworthy business owner. If you incorporate a "full transparency with a need-to-know" component, they will pay attention when you communicate to them directly. They will know your style and that "this" must be important. That kind of strategic communication protects your business.

Target and Timing for Go Big Program Announcements

In the last chapter, you sketched out a few Leadership Go Big plans for clients, staff, and the community. Now it's time to design a general communication process that ensures your three key targets understand what you are going to do *for them* this year and why they should care. This is yours to set up, control, and spin. Make it count so that your leadership capital is well spent. Your investment needs to hit the mark.

I recommend streamlining where you can, even though your target audiences are separate entities. Perhaps you focus on using the same timeframes but with a different message for each target. I have outlined one plan below to give you a basic idea of the five basic steps involved in a hypothetical communication plan. This one starts at the beginning of the calendar year, but you can modify it to your own schedule.

Step 1: January

Go Big Pre-Announcement(s) – Announce Early = Smart Offense

- **Purpose:** Remind clients/employees you value their business/ employment and want to maintain their loyalty and support this year.
- **Tactics:** Create curiosity and build anticipation. Get the targets' immediate attention. Consider giving the plan a catchy name. Provide general details and time frame as appropriate. Go wide with your existing communication modes, including social media. This "coming soon" messaging serves an offensive purpose by keeping potential clients from looking at other vendors or service providers, and keeping employees from thinking about switching jobs.

Step 2: February/March

Announcement – Details and Start (What, When, How, Why)

- **Purpose:** Program kick-off to generate interest and action
- **Tactics:** Make this announcement engaging and as interesting as possible. Include specifics about what you are doing or offering and the ways they will benefit. Include details and time frame. Go wide with your existing communication modes including social media. Provide more detail including your phone number and email to answer any further questions. Re-state that you are very pleased to be able to offer this change, additional service, new educational program, or client workshop and why. Close with an upbeat message.

Step 3: May/June

Build Momentum

- **Purpose:** Show your commitment to the program by providing this update, progress report, anecdotal success story, and positive outlook for the coming months.
- **Tactics:** This may require that you spin the results a bit if it's slow to catch on. This is a program that you have committed to for one year, and many consumers and clients are not early adopters. Do not show weakness by being discouraged. You are a leader. Review the program in

brief, the benefits, and a call to action, with a special offer if appropriate. Share a client or staff testimonial that backs up the positive attributes of participation—especially strong if it's a person with influence.

Step 4: September/October

Final Push

- **Purpose:** Reward current participants and make it easy for others to jump into the program.
- **Tactics:** By now, your Go Big Plan is established and doing well. Give a brief update including any changes, and a reminder that the opportunity to participate is open and re-state the benefits. If time is running out to participate, say it. If you have a second program to add or an addition to the existing program, hype it. Set a positive tone for the newest program and provide a few details and another testimonial. Give them an incentive to get in, act now, and be a part of what's happening. Ask for feedback and provide your phone number. It will soon be time to evaluate this program for its merits in order to determine whether you will continue it next year. Make a final hard push, but don't sound desperate if it has not gone as you'd hoped.

Step 5: December

End-of-the-Year Thank You, Reminder, and Wrap-Up

- **Purpose:** To remind everyone, especially those who have not participated, that you did something meaningful *for* them that displayed leadership because you are committed and you *care*.
- **Tactics:** Thank everyone for their business, their employment, or the support of the community. Subtly remind them what new programs you implemented and that you hope they found these beneficial and meaningful. Wish everyone Happy Holidays and say you look forward to sharing plans in January for another year of working together.

COMMUNICATION PLAN EXERCISE

Outline a basic communication plan for announcing one of your new Go Big programs from the previous chapter. Include these elements:

My Go Big Plan

- Purpose – What are you trying to accomplish?

  _____

  _____

- Who – Which group are you targeting?

  _____

  _____

- What – What is the basic plan?

  _____

  _____

- Why – What will the target gain?

  _____

  _____

- When – What is your time frame? How much time do you need to prepare? When can you pre-announce? How frequently should you provide updates? Monthly? Bi-monthly? Quarterly?

  _____

  _____

Program Details

- Kickoff

  _____

  _____

- Duration

  _____

  _____

- Launch

  _____

_____

- Update schedule

_____

_____

Communication Plan

- Which modes will you use to launch and update the plan?

  _____

  _____

- When will you have a staff meeting about it, and what will you say?

  _____

  _____

- How will you use social media, and who will be responsible for that?

  _____

  _____

- What kinds of collateral or promotional materials will you need?

  _____

  _____

- Where will you display your materials and how and when will they be distributed?

  _____

  _____

Strategic Leaders know rock-solid, well-planned communication keeps their businesses on track and helps protect it by creating an environment of trust and security. This chapter covered the basics of what should be considered essential for creating a communication plan and a checklist to make sure you have the breadth and width to ensure your messages are consistently received and effective.

This is never more important than when things go wrong. As the owner, this responsibility falls squarely on your shoulders in good times and bad. People, *your* people, want to know what's going on, and they want to hear it from *you*.

In the next chapter, we look at how to lead strategically when bad things happen—because like it or not, they can *and do*.

CHAPTER 9

What to Do When
Bad Things Happen

Owning restaurants and hotels means we deal with many different customer profiles, on top of being open seven days and nights a week. Basically, we are always on notice. Our customer-centric approach is this: When a mistake occurs, own up to it very quickly, very directly, and at the highest management level possible. That way we meet our clients' high expectations even if we can't always control what happened.

Shirin Kanji

Tampa, Florida
Senior Vice President and Chief Investment Officer, Impact Properties
President of Impact's Retail Division
BurgerFi multi-unit franchisee, multi-brand franchisee

What's the worst thing that could happen to your business? I'm not talking about the thing that keeps you up at night, like making payroll or deciding to terminate someone you were counting on. I'm talking about the nightmare thing. *That* thing.

All business owners, including franchisors and franchisees, have a "worst thing that could happen" scenario they carry with them. We all know what our "worst thing" is. We just don't even want to think about it. I resolve to be the first person, maybe the *only* person, to tell you that you need to address your "worst thing" this year. It's time.

Why? Because bad things can and *do* happen. No brand, franchisee, or corporate entity is immune, and that includes yours. Remember what happened to the reputation and stock of fast casual darling Chipotle in 2016 after a salmonella outbreak in the company's supply chain? And analysts say Target has still not recovered entirely from the computer hack that compromised more than 40 million customer credit cards at the height of the holiday season in 2013. You *know* United Airlines CEO Oscar Muñoz wishes he had gotten in front of the public outcry that followed the infamous video showing a passenger being dragged off a plane in early 2017. In fact, I'll bet the entire airline industry wishes that he did, too. What happens to one impacts the whole segment, and public trust is vital to everyone's success.

While these are not franchise examples, our industry is just as vulnerable to 24-hour mass media platforms and news cycles as large corporations—maybe even more so. That's because the structure of our business model decentralizes the ownership and thereby spreads the brand-damaging risks, and responsibilities, to all franchise holders.

You can show your strategic leadership by pondering, planning, and preventing bad things from happening. I've shared a number of bad things that did happen in my business over the fifteen years I owned and operated my franchise. Fortunately, I learned quickly how to respond and contain many of them, thanks to some early advice from my franchisor. Later, after some hard lessons learned, I developed and implemented prevention and protection strategies to eliminate others.

Here is a quick list of the top five nightmare scenarios for the early childhood industry:

1. Leaving a child on a bus
2. Leaving a child locked in your building after hours
3. Having a staff member accused of molestation
4. Having a child in your care suffer a life-threatening injury
5. Sustaining a vehicle running into your building or playground

My personal nightmare? Someone drops a baby. This *haunted* me.

PREVENTION EXERCISE

Now it's your turn. List the top five worst scenarios that could happen to your business.

1. _____
2. _____
3. _____
4. _____
5. _____

Keep your list in mind as you read this chapter. By the end, you should feel confident enough to tackle at least one or two of these this year. That means two fewer things to worry about, which gives you more time and energy to focus on growing your revenue and enjoying your business because you chose to lead strategically.

Before we jump into prevention, let's discuss responsibility. Specifically, who is responsible when bad things happen? Is it you, the franchisee, or your franchisor? In order to add some context to this question, take another look at your list. Did it include acts of God, such as hurricanes, earthquakes, and tornadoes? Hurricane Harvey was creating decimating destruction and hardship in Southeast Texas just as this book was going to press. What about issues that pertain to supply chain management, such as contaminated food, unfavorable health inspections, or the myriad licensing issues that play a role in so many franchise operations?

So, who *is* responsible? Hopefully, your answer was "both." You are in this together. It's not only your franchisor's responsibility to keep you out of harm's way. It's yours, too. And ignorance is not bliss. Your franchisor probably offers support and training for many of your industry's worst-case scenarios, but you are responsible for asking.

If you aren't aware, find out. If you aren't satisfied and your franchise has a Franchisee Advisory Committee (FAC), tell your committee representative you are working on strategies to protect your business and request that the FAC focus on that topic this year. Or suggest it be a topic at your next annual meeting and offer to participate by leading a breakout group with franchisees and corporate folks to get this started. Hearing about worst-case scenarios in the news causes everyone to hold their collective breath. It's likely most of the people in your franchise system will welcome the idea of getting this conversation started or getting it to a deeper level before something happens.

Here are a few prevention strategies that you can develop, enhance, or implement this year to protect your business.

Use Resources and Reinforce Risk Management

Like building loyalty, protection is strategically layered over the years. You pay the first three resources on this list whether you ask for their help and advice or not. It's time to ask.

Franchisor – Start by scheduling a meeting with your franchise representative and explain that you are looking for resources to better help you protect your business. What has been developed internally? What experience with other franchisees can they share? Also, search for best practices in your industry. Invest the time it takes to gather all of the information you can find before you get too far into your planning. You'll save time, and maybe your business, by doing so.

Liability Insurance – As you'll learn in Pillar 3, Money Metrics, I had an employee who stole more than $40,000 from my business. (Yes, really.) My liability insurance policy, unbeknownst to me, had a rider that covered thefts. In the annual review following this very distressing revelation and stressful period, my liability agent, who specialized in the childcare industry, reminded me about the rider and promptly had a $20,000 check issued the next week, which helped bring closure. Does your insurer specialize in your segment and conduct an annual review? I was grateful that he insisted we have a review every single year and considered him a valuable resource.

Workers' Compensation (WC) Insurance – This is required insurance, but who you get it from is up to you. Even if you use a payroll processing company, you can exclude this and contract with a WC specialist as long as you do not have an employee leasing arrangement. Regardless of your provider, you should ask for and expect regular support including training, a site review, and an annual meeting. Once a year, a workers' compensation safety specialist *who understood my business* gave a presentation during a staff meeting. In addition to reviewing our injuries from the past year (without naming names or citing fault), she made numerous suggestions and challenged us to have a safer workplace. It was valuable to have a third party explain that in addition to protecting our insurance rate and giving the company more money to spend on things like raises, a safer workplace can prevent an injury that can be a huge setback for an employee and his or her family.

Employment Attorney – An experienced employment attorney is well worth his or her hourly rate. The biggest mistake you could make, other than not having one on retainer, is waiting too long to call them when you have a problem. Over time, you'll get good at handling 80 percent of the problems that come up. The other 20 percent can be put to rest with a 30-minute phone call. On an annual basis, that's a call or two a year. I shared in a previous chapter about having to terminate one of my favorite managers for showing favoritism. Because I had consulted my attorney several weeks in advance, I knew when it was time to make that decision and how best to implement it. That same attorney helped me walk a tight rope when I had a long-term WC case with another valuable employee. To my knowledge, she is still employed at my former franchise. I attribute that to having sound legal advice and following it. Start by asking your franchisor who he or she recommends. Many firms are national, and you may have an office in your city or a national account relationship established.

Public Relations Agent – A crisis management public relations professional should also be on retainer. Your goal, should something bad happen, is to stay under the media radar. Barring that, a professional public relations agency can help you keep the news cycle short and address the issue quickly. I saw how effective this could be when I learned about a franchise owner and friend had one of the childcare nightmare scenarios happen at his franchise. Fortunately, his daughter was a PR professional. Within hours, she had crafted a well-written response explaining the unusual circumstance, what was being done to ensure this never occurred again, and that, thankfully, no one had been harmed. The statement closed with the center owner taking full responsibility. Within hours, the news station aired her entire written response. The news value of the nightmare was over in less than 24 hours. Contrast that to my experience with no PR agent. When Stingray Boy got on the wrong bus, my story was news for well over two of the longest days of my life.

Human Resources Trainer – Twice a year, the owner of the benefits administration company I contracted with provided a human resources lunch and learn for all center managers and supervisors. She covered topics such as how to terminate an employee, how to screen employees, and why documentation is important. I'm sure her training kept me out of hot water, and I kept her as my agent for 10 years, in large part because she helped protect my business by reducing the likelihood of being sued.

When it comes to insurance, I recommend finding experienced representatives who are knowledgeable about your segment and are passionate and engaged enough to jump at the opportunity to assist you. If the liability and workers' comp insurance carriers and agents seem reluctant to help you, then find others who will.

One final note about selecting professionals: When you are in the early years of ownership, it behooves you to work with the agents and professionals who know your franchise system well. In most cases, your franchisor will recommend you contact professionals used by other franchisees, and this is sound advice. Over time, especially if you are unable to have face-to-face meetings with them because of geographic limitations, you may want to consider local agents and professionals who know your state laws and your market segment. In other words, the corporate association becomes less of a factor as you gain experience and the service you receive becomes more important.

Strategic Leadership for Risk Management

Here is a basic five-step outline you might find helpful if you're ready to incorporate risk management and prevention into your strategic leadership plan. If you completed the exercise in the beginning of the chapter, you've already done the first step.

1. **Make a list of the possible nightmare scenarios.** Don't forget the most frequent acts of God in your area of the country. Three back-to-back hurricanes rolled through Central Florida in 2004. We did not sustain

any major damage, but it was tough on cash flow and everyone's nerves. Especially mine. That's when I got serious about protecting my business.

2. **Choose the two most plausible, urgent, or damaging scenarios and assign a time frame to roll out a plan for each one.** Put the remainder on next year's list. (Bad things have no calendar). You will probably find the process you put together can be used for other scenarios.

3. **Communicate to your staff and franchisor that you are addressing these specific scenarios over the coming year.** Solicit or assign a leader to be the point person who will assist you and help others understand why this is important for the business and therefore for them.

4. **Consider all possible internal and external resources.** These include other businesses that may have been through similar situations. These resources can help you formulate a plan for each of the scenarios you chose. This is not time to hold back. Ask questions.

5. **Start your research and then get to work.** Once you get started, the rest will flow more easily than you anticipated.

Let me be the first to congratulate you on being the kind of strategic leader who recognizes that risk management is an important part of your job. Your decision to better protect your business and commit the time to doing so is not the easy choice. But it is the right choice.

As for me and my worst nightmare scenario? No, thank goodness, no one ever dropped a baby.

In this section, we focused on **Pillar 2: Strategic Leadership – Protect Your Business**. Being the kind of leader your business needs and the kind of leader you want to be is an investment that takes time, planning, and discipline to achieve. You are showing you're willing to do that because you're developing your knowledge and expertise by reading this book and working through the exercises.

I hope you are now vividly picturing yourself as a franchisee in the top 10 percent to 20 percent of your system because you are well on your way. With leadership strategies in process, it's time to talk money. Specifically, **Pillar 3: Money Metrics – Grow Your Business**.

Placing this sign and then breaking ground were both major causes for celebration.

Roland, my ever-present side-kick, and I doing our own brand of surveying.

Framing *finished*; I exhaled.

Everyone needs a break, even when your feet don't quite touch the ground!

FINANCIAL FORECAST AND ANALYSIS - YEAR ONE-START FALL '98

Month Number + Weeks/Month	1 5	2 4	3 4	4 5	5 4	6 4	7 5	8 4	9 4	10 5	11 4	12 4	Total # #
Revenue:	50,500	52,700	64,200	89,250	88,600	98,100	95,250	119,600	95,250	119,600	95,250	95,250	1,052,150
# of Children	140	155	180	210	240	260	280	280	280	280	280	280	
# of Instructors	14	16	18	21	24	27	28	28	28	28	28	28	

Expenses:
Salaries & Wages:
Director &

Owner	5,750	4,600	4,600	5,750	4,600	4,600	4,010	5,750	4,010	5,750	4,600	4,600	59,500
Assistant Director	1,700	1,360	1,360	1,700	1,360	1,360	1,360	1,700	1,360	1,360	1,360	1,360	17,940
Food Preparer	1,500	1,200	1,205	1,500	1,200	1,200	1,200	1,500	1,200	1,500	1,200	1,200	15,600
Instructors	19,600	17,870	20,160	29,400	26,880	30,240	31,360	39,200	31,360	39,200	31,360	31,360	349,840
Payroll Taxes	3,183	2,790	3,046	4,276	3,794	4,176	4,209	5,374	4,209	5,374	4,299	4,299	49,214
Total Salaries & Wages	31,733	27,870	30,356	42,626	37,839	41,570	42,830	53,574	42,859	53,574	42,859	42,859	490,594

Other Expenses:

Advertising	150	150	150	150	150	150	150	150	150	150	150	150	1,800
Amortization	236	236	236	236	236	236	236	236	236	236	236	236	2,832
Auto Expense	1,700	1,700	1,700	1,700	1,700	1,700	1,700	1,700	1,700	1,700	1,700	1,700	20,400
Cleaning & Linen	1,250	1,250	1,250	1,250	1,250	1,250	1,250	1,250	1,250	1,250	1,250	1,250	15,000
Co-op Advertising													
Depreciation	2,636	2,636	2,636	2,636	2,636	636	2,636	2,636	2,636	2,636	2,636	2,636	31,564
Fuel	1,500	1,359	1,394	1,370	1,372	1,325	1,368	1,500	1,290	1,500	1,290	1,200	16,530
Furniture Lease	3,000	3,000	3,000	3,000	3,000	3,000	3,000	3,000	3,000	3,000	1,006	3,000	36,006
Franchise Royalty	2,975	2,625	3,060	4,463	4,400	4,905	4,760	5,980	4,760	4,760	4,760	4,760	52,658
Interest on Long Term	10,050	10,016	10,082	9,988	9,971	9,950	9,888	9,925	9,915	8,900	9,884	9,865	119,416
Debt (mortgage)													
Interest on S/T Note	1,727	1,727	1,723	1,727	1,727	1,727	1,723	1,727	1,727	1,727	1,727	1,727	20,728
Legal & Accounting	500	500	500	500	500	500	500	500	500	500	500	500	6,000
Liability Insurance	1,200	1,200	1,200	1,200	1,200	1,200	1,200	1,200	1,200	1,200	1,200	1,200	14,400
Miscellaneous	200	200	200	200	200	200	200	200	200	200	200	200	2,400
Officer's Life Insurance	53	53	53	53	53	53	53	53	53	53	53	53	636
Paper Goods	373	332	348	410	341	351	317	375	305	375	305	396	4,134
Special Programs	100	100	100	100	100	100	100	100	100	100	100	100	1,200
Repair & Maintenance	250	250	250	250	250	250	250	250	250	250	250	250	3,000
Supplies	150	150	150	150	150	150	150	150	150	150	150	150	1,800
Taxes & Licenses	2,200	2,200	2,200	2,200	2,200	2,200	2,200	2,200	2,200	2,200	2,200	2,200	26,400
Utilities	1,200	1,500	1,200	1,500	1,500	1,200	1,200	1,200	1,500	1,200	1,500	1,200	15,600
Total Other Expenses	31,727	30,858	31,350	33,184	32,354	22,666	32,835	34,604	33,721	34,571	32,691	32,675	392,492
Total Expenses	63,460	58,723	61,710	76,110	70,149	71,236	75,695	88,175	75,580	88,145	75,525	75,525	883,086
Net Book Income	(3,960)	(6,015)	(555)	13,140	11,851	17,864	19,505	30,825	19,620	30,855	19,650	19,665	770,064

CHRISTY'S KIDS, INC.
CAPITAL AND PRE-OPENING COSTS

CPIT		$80,000
FRANCHISE FEE		$37,500
PROPERTY		$305,500
Land	$157,500	
Site Work	140,000	
Utilities	8,000	
SOFT COSTS		$190,000
County Fees	120,000	
Engineering Fees	50,000	
Attorney & CPA	20,000	
HARD COSTS		$965,000
Building &		
Construction	930,000	
(contingency)	20,000	
Landscaping	15,000	
FURNITURE		$169,500
& EQUIPMENT		
BUS		$ 80,000
TOTAL PROJECT COST		$1,827,500
PERSONAL CASH CONTRIBUTED		260,000

AMOUNT OF LOAN REQUESTED FOR PURPOSES OF
LEASING/FINANCING THE EQUIPMENT AND THE BUS
IS $250,000.

This is the actual business plan that I lived by for the first three years.

A well-worn page from the plan showing construction and start-up costs.

Look closely at the wheels on the car. My hubcaps were stolen three times after moving into the apartment complex. The third time, Roland and I *both* cried.

Construction done and ready to open!

This is the main building as it looks today.

Low cost and consistent client loyalty building - Parent Appreciation coffee set-up.

I received this card from my staff following a casino holiday party.

Mr. Skip was our much beloved facilities maintenance manager who retired.

That cow was a welcomed and a frequent guest at my franchise.

Balloon Day was one of our favorite days of the year!

This "sweet-spot" medallion was presented to each Pre-K graduate who began in Suite 100, the infant room.

Joy and Steven Silvers won the top franchisee award that year. Linda McCart, holding the plaque in the center was also their Quality Assurance representative.

Julie Moyes, a franchisee in North Carolina along with her husband Brooks, celebrated at a franchisor party in the early years.

My Mother, Mary Ann Blessing, was my frequent date for corporate award events and parties.

Enrichment Center expansion was
ambitious but much easier compared to
the first build out.

Corporate Quality Assurance Rep
Linda McCart attended the Enrichment
Center pre-opening event.

The Enrichment Center
as it looks today.

Monument sign and fencing provided
the academy campus image I wanted
for my franchise.

Final expansion was opening up in
neighboring Avalon Park community.

I made many friends while researching and writing this book,
including this clever Circle K recruitment bear!

Shannon Kemp and her Style
Encore staff were preparing for their
anniversary celebration event the day
we met for our interview.

Eddie Titen and his Sonny's BBQ team
enjoy giving back by serving others
from Eddie's very cool truck.

Kevin Wray, Peterbrooke Chocolatier franchisee explains to a class of
Rollins College business students why dedication and passion are required
to be a successful small business owner.

A debt of gratitude paid to Pat and
Janice Vinson, founders of Kids 'R' Kids
Academies for guiding me to success.
Photo credit Tori Grace Barnwell

Like you, reading about experiences
helps me evolve, get motivated and
stay focused. Keep reading!

MONEY METRICS

Grow Your Business

At the heart of it, this book is about growing your business and making the money that equates to your definition of success each year. The unvarnished truth? If you want to grow your business and make money consistently, you have to know your numbers. I mean *really* know your numbers—inside and out, backward and forward, in your sleep and during every waking moment. Actually, you need to know more than your numbers. You need to know your metrics.

I have an advanced business degree and still looked up the definition for metrics so I wouldn't embarrass myself. In business, a metric is a quantifiable measure used to track, monitor, and assess the success or failure of programs and processes. Metrics are the tools used to set goals for your business and to track your progress toward those goals, and they're represented by ratios, percentages, dollars, and other measurements.

Metrics are important because you need as much information as you can access in order to understand your baseline and create a plan for growth. Knowing how well you are, or are not, doing in specific areas such as payroll or food costs gives you the best insight on where to start. I call this pillar Money Metrics because you're going to learn how to take action to monetize that knowledge.

We'll start building this pillar with *your* franchisor numbers, *your* industry numbers, and *your* franchisee numbers. You don't need this information right now. I'll keep it easy by using mine, but before long, you will need them if you want to be a high-performing franchisee. Comparing your metrics to those of successful franchisees in your system is excellent way to gauge what you are doing well and where the best opportunities for improvement lie. Industry data may be harder to come by, but worth the effort if you can incorporate it.

When you bought a franchise, you also bought franchise metrics that come with it. They may have been tucked into your training manual and need updating, or you might need to ask for this information. Fair warning: Some franchisors compile better data than others. Be sure to politely let your franchisor know you are seeking this information to better your business.

After metrics, we will look closely at what drives your profit and how you grow revenue each year. We will start by focusing on the two measures that directly impact your income: top- and bottom-line expenses and revenue. We'll examine ways to reduce your three biggest expense categories and how to increase your revenue so your profits grow. And finally, we'll cover how to build and maintain a true competitive advantage to ensure your customers keep coming back.

Understanding, building, and using Money Metrics knowledge to grow your business is the most productive way to get exactly where you want to be as a franchise owner this year. My goal is to get you into the next performance tier of your system, and then the next one after that, until you permanently reside in the top 10 to 20 percent. No more 80 percent for you. Ready? Let's go!

CHAPTER 10

Know Your Numbers

Over time, I found myself spending more time in the metrics and numbers as my business grew, and less time with the people. One day, I woke up and realized I wasn't enjoying what I was doing, and my top- and bottom-line numbers weren't growing like I was used to seeing. And then it hit me: I wasn't focusing my time on the one thing responsible for all my metric success—the people delivering the services, having the right people on the team, and making sure they were being nurtured, feeling cared for, being well-trained, and as a result truly excited about the brand. Once I shifted to a healthier balance of focusing on the guest experience, the team experience, and the overall mood in the business, and then the metrics, great things started happening again.

Tim Bradbury

Sacramento, California
European Wax Center franchisee since 2005
Five-store multi-unit franchisee and area representative

've been known to characterize the 4 Pillars Approach as representing the less-tangible, or softer, aspects of running a franchise because they aren't typically found in the franchise operations manual. But let's be honest. What could be more tangible than talking about money? Specifically, your money? And truth be told, deciding to intimately know your numbers can be daunting, even a little bit scary, and that's understandable. However, this is a critical pillar for growing your business, so take a deep breath and even a step back to prepare for this challenge.

Then sit back down and get ready to dig in. This is an extremely worthwhile investment of your time, and I promise to make this as painless as possible.

The reward? Once you get a firm grasp on your Money Metrics, you will find renewed motivation and the confidence to be the successful franchise owner you want to be. Better still, your plan for the year will start to take shape right before your eyes and you'll see your path to the next tier.

The 3 Levels of 'Knowing'

When it comes to understanding your Money Metrics, there are three distinct levels of knowing. These levels were adapted for business from a Situational Awareness (SA) model developed by Mica R. Endsley in 1995 for training military pilots. I review this each semester with business students as part of their introduction to Market Place Live, a computer-simulated business competition, and have found it to be the best way to explain the concept and importance of knowing your money metrics.

Level 1 – Perception

You know your weekly and monthly revenue expense numbers. You also should know which expenses you have during the year that are quarterly or annual such as advertising contributions or property taxes. You have these formatted by month, by quarter, and for the year. These raw numbers are extremely valuable, especially as you start to identify quarterly revenue and expense trends.

Perception starts by determining what reports and data you need on hand. You may be surprised, as I was, by the amount of data you have at your fingertips. Our franchise operating software, which we used for everything except my personal company bookkeeping, compiled useful information that could be formatted daily, weekly, monthly, and annually. I recommend thumbing through your User Guide, specifically the Reports section of your franchise operating software, or calling your franchise software point person before you get started. Unless you are a brand-new franchise owner, you need at least one full calendar year of data. I usually had the past three years available when I did my annual review and planning.

PERCEPTION EXERCISE

List the reports and information you need to have on hand to form a basic understanding of your revenue and expense numbers.

1. _____

2. _____

3. _____

Level 2 – Comprehension

You know what each expense is as a percentage of your revenue and how they each impact your bottom line monthly, quarterly, and annually. You also know the target percentages for the major expense categories for your industry and for the top-performing franchisees (TPFs) within your franchise system. You can gather this information by talking to your franchisor and to other franchise owners. You need both perspectives. Also, go outside the system and research another similar franchise system and one independent business that is successful in your industry. (I was a member of a local childcare director's organization and gained valuable metric data from other members). You now have up to four sources to compare: your numbers, your franchisor numbers, a TPF number, and an industry number outside of your system.

While perception is based on raw numbers, comprehension is based on percentages. This allows you to understand how the large and small expenses and metrics of your business impact your profit on an annual basis. Look at these percentages against the previous year(s) and compare them to franchisor and industry data. When viewed in this way, the true cost of your benefits, marketing, and other programs can start to be viewed strategically. Sometimes it can be rather shocking to see how much you spend on "necessary" and routine expenses. And the opposite is also true. You may not spend enough on payroll and decide it's a perfect time to increase your starting pay to or enhance your service by adding another staff member.

COMPREHENSION EXERCISE

List three significant expense items you want to know as a percentage of your monthly revenue that you currently do not know.

1. _____

2. _____

3. _____

Level 3 – Projection

You are able to project into the future how any change in a revenue or expense number impacts the other numbers and specifically how any change impacts your profit. You understand fully how they interact.

Projection starts when you have sufficiently mastered perception and comprehension. Projection is the goal, but to get there you must start with a baseline (your current metrics) and a target percentage (industry and TPFs metrics). Without those, projecting changes in the numbers is not going to be fruitful. You know how much money is coming in, where it came from, what you had to spend to bring it in, and what was left.

For example, you know the sales incentive you put in place for your front-line people to kick off the new service your franchisor unveiled at the annual conference will cost you about five percent of your anticipated 10 percent revenue increase. The highly anticipated new service is sure to bring in several new Sweet Spot Clients, which equates to an increase of $650 a week or $2,800 monthly, and an annual revenue gain of $33,800. According to this projection, you will spend $1,690 on the incentives that generated $33,800 in incremental revenue. If your profit margin is twenty-three percent, you will make an additional $7,400 this year. By the second quarter you knew it was working as planned and you turned your attention to another opportunity.

Level 3 knowledge is critical to growing your business. As a Kids 'R' Kids franchisee, I valued the weekly classroom waiting list report almost as much as I did the deposit report. Like most franchise segments, there was a normal rate of attrition inherent with clients due to a variety of reasons. Couples divorced, moved, or got laid off and no longer needed our services. For this reason, a "healthy" waiting list was very important to ensure revenue stayed consistent. Without it, revenue would be forfeited while managers tried to fill spots when someone left.

With Level 3 knowledge, I was able to peg the appropriate and best number for each classroom waiting list (too many and it hurt the collective goodwill with those who were waiting). Having an active waiting list and knowing the right numbers by specific age group and classroom allowed me to accurately predict the revenue. If the waiting list was inadequate to sustain the growth I was planning, I knew that in advance and could implement a new client marketing plan and alert staff to a possible decrease in hours.

PROJECTION EXERCISE

List three areas of your business that you will target for projection data development. Specify how often this data should be updated and reviewed for the specific projection you are targeting.

Example: Maximize enrollment revenue / update waiting list weekly / review weekly

Data Objective	Report Description	Review Frequency

Your goal is to get to Level 3 *and stay there*. Level 3 knowledge is very powerful. Having Level 3 knowledge will ensure you can strengthen, protect, and grow your business every year. For most franchisees, getting to Level 3 will require spending some significant quality time with reports and data in order to really grasp how areas of your business impact other areas and your profit for the year. The more you dig in, the more questions you will have. Go ahead and ask them.

Ask a Lot of Questions

John Maxwell, the author of *Good Leaders Ask Great Questions: Your Foundation for Successful Leadership* and 40 other business management books, believes it is a good practice to regularly ask your staff questions about the numbers. I did this regularly and found my staff quite eager to answer my questions once they understood my motivation. They liked helping me to be a better planner, and your team will, too. It gave them an opportunity to show they knew what was going on with the business. That's all kinds of good for employee morale and career development. Synergy bonus intact.

How does knowing your metrics and asking questions work in a real-world situation?

Scenario #1

You own a hardware store franchise and notice when you do your monthly review that your profit for February is down by $5,300 compared with last year's number. You dig in and see expenses are unusually high. You dig further and learn your manager placed your semi-annual mulch and garden sale order in early February so you would be ready for the March sales event. Unfortunately, he ordered too early and now the bill has been paid but the revenue won't come in until late March. Cash flow crunch is problem #1. Problem #2 is the profit number didn't reflect that your recent involvement with the Rotary Club had brought in several new clients in February. Luckily, in your monthly review, you also compared the revenue number against the previous year and saw it was $1,800 higher. You then asked questions and learned several club members stopped in and bought some bigger-ticket items over the last few weeks.

In this example, knowing your numbers revealed that you need to smooth out your cash flow; not that your profit is down as compared to the previous year.

You learned that your community involvement was indeed paying dividends and vowed to make the next monthly meeting.

Scenario #2

You own a buffet-style restaurant franchise and notice when you do your monthly review that your payroll number is low as a percentage of revenue. Of course, that's not necessarily a bad thing. However, you are concerned because this is unusual and you want to make sure the guest experience was not compromised. You start asking questions and learn that Little League started up last Saturday and 30 families descended on your establishment when you were not on-site. (The weekend manager neglected to mention this). Of course, you'll want to be well-staffed next Saturday and maybe add two team members to help in the kitchen and bus tables. Why? Because you saw this as an opportunity, contacted the Little League, and hand-delivered some coupons to the coaches during practice last week.

In this example, if you hadn't taken the time to do a proper and timely financial review of your numbers, you would have missed this opportunity to generate additional revenue for your restaurant and, worse, may have presented guests with less-than-stellar service.

This is exactly how knowing your numbers can help you improve your operation, enhance service, and grow your revenue and profits. You may have noticed that each example referenced a monthly review. Looking at your metrics on a consistent basis is critical.

Incorporate Regular Metric Reviews

Monthly: I made a habit of going to the office one Sunday afternoon each month to just "play with the numbers." This way I encountered no interruptions and no pressure. I recommend finding a similar dedicated time that works for you and then be extremely disciplined about getting there and focusing on the numbers. Afterward, you can reward yourself, as I did, by doing something you really enjoy like going out for a nice meal or a movie to shift back out of work mode.

Quarterly: I recommend doing comparisons to previous quarters to ensure your programs are getting the results you want. I did this consistently over the course of ownership, and it made a huge difference in my motivation, my confidence, and most importantly my results.

I believe those dedicated hours, spent focused solely on the numbers each month got me and kept me in the top tier of my franchise system. It's that important.

Can't Find or Make the Time?

I can hear you now. "Christy, who has the time for all this number crunching?" My answer: "What could be more important in your business than knowing how your business is doing?" If you can't get motivated to set aside the time necessary to dig in and really understand your numbers, you might consider reframing the task. Here are a few tricks I used to keep myself motivated to stay on top of my numbers that might work for you.

- **Find money!** When I did the metrics "dive," I always found things the business could do without or services we were simply not taking advantage of (or even using) and thus "found" money. Canceling services you don't use feels good, saves money, and shows your staff you know the details and are on top of your business. They, in turn, will follow your lead.
- **Multitask.** As long as you are reviewing your expenses, pull out your vendor files and review the recent invoices against your most recent contract. Call or email your vendors and say you are doing a review and want to know how they can "do better" or "do more" or "cost less" in order for them to maintain your business or earn it for another year. If you want to play hardball, or aren't satisfied, get a second or third quote. Vendors, suppliers, and service providers find creative ways to increase prices, sometimes without your knowledge.
- **Pay yourself.** I used my monthly reviews as a time to pay myself a distribution check for the month. That helped keep me on task and was a fitting reward for working on a Sunday afternoon. Then came the fattening meal or round of golf to celebrate another profitable month.

The Importance of Level 3 Knowledge and Discipline

I'm sharing this next very difficult story because it's important you know I had many struggles along this journey, perhaps like you are having now. We all have days and weeks when we wonder, *What am I doing this for?* However, some down periods are worse than others. This one was pretty bad and should further emphasize the importance of getting to Level 3 knowledge and being disciplined about staying focused on your numbers each month.

Thief in My Franchise

At the end of 2004, I decided to bump up my residence a notch or two. It was time to get out of the small home I had purchased post-apartment. I was steeped in the closing and moving process when I went for my annual mammogram and learned I had early stage breast cancer. I was upset, of course, but not derailed from the seemingly more important things I was so intent on doing. Until I was.

The surgery and daily treatments wiped me out, and for the first time I was dependent on others to oversee the center. I was overwhelmed by the support and love I received and was grateful to the management team for handling the day-to-day. I came into the office each morning and did what I needed to do before heading to the clinic for the daily dose of radiation. On top of being worried and tired, I was distracted by two house closings and the upcoming move. In short, I was stressed out, vulnerable, and trusting. A very bad combination.

It wasn't until midsummer that I discovered a very trusted employee of eight years had been stealing from me. It had started at least a year before I was diagnosed and I had totally missed it. She got serious when I had less time at the office. By shorting a cash deposit here, and disguising a payment there, this person had stolen more than $40,000 by the time she was dismissed.

How could this happen if I was operating as a Level 3 owner? Fair question, and one I asked myself for months.

I'm going to tell you everything so you can decide for yourself and hopefully prevent this from happening in your business.

Clearly, I didn't dig deep enough or ask enough hard questions when periodically the numbers weren't quite adding up.

First, in order to stop her, I needed to suspect someone was stealing, and I did not. Second, to get to the point where I knew for certain money was missing, I would have to go through every deposit every single day and match it to the payment and the account entry. I didn't do that either. Third, the monthly revenue continued to grow and I continued to work my Sunday afternoon each month. Sometimes my intuition was screaming at me that something was wrong. Still, I didn't listen. It never once occurred to me someone might be stealing. I thought it was me and that I wasn't able to manage the accounting well enough, and that was at least partially true. I could have caught it.

This is what I think. My business had gotten too complicated too fast. Between the credit card terminals, electronic transfers, cash, checks, State of Florida payments, and automatic payments, I couldn't keep track well enough to catch the well-timed omissions from the overall balance. I was performing random checks on deposits instead of detailed, methodical, thorough reviews of all deposits and statements.

It wasn't until after she was terminated and I spend weeks with boxes of deposit slips and reports covering my dining room table that I saw the pattern. She struck most often when I was out of town and out of the office. The period when I was dealing with my health issues was particularly bad. Big ouch. It really hurt.

As embarrassing and depressing as it was and still is to admit, I know it could have gone on longer and been even worse. Employee theft is rampant and one of many reasons it's important to really know your numbers. Over the next seven years, I caught two other people stealing from me. While these were low-level thefts and did not involve tuition money, I had learned to watch in a different way, and so incurred minimal losses. As you now know, I learned the hard way, but I learned and that's why I needed to share this painful story with you.

My experience is not an isolated one. Not long ago I was discussing this book with an Air BnB guest who stayed in my garage apartment for several nights. This gentleman was a retired accountant and volunteered the following story about his good friend, also an accountant, who had bought an existing fast-food franchise of a well-known national brand. Apparently, the new franchisee put off going to the training and then, months into ownership, was frustrated and upset he was not making the amount of money he had expected. Upon digging, the vulnerable new franchise owner learned his store manager had been stealing $2,500 a week. Thieves know when and where we are weak, and this one struck hard and fast. The new franchisee had postponed attending owner training and therefore was not as familiar with the system as he might have been. The store manager knew this and knew the system.

I don't want this to happen to you. The more you know and can project your numbers based on the metrics you develop, the less likely you are to be preyed upon. Stay diligent and dig deep when something doesn't look right, and absolutely don't ignore your intuition.

Once you have established your baselines for your metrics and are able to perceive, comprehend, and project your numbers, you will be able to fine-tune your business. By fine-tuning, I mean cutting and trimming expenses and growing your revenue, both of which result in increased profits for you.

We'll start with looking at your expenses. This side of the profit equation is often overlooked, but the 4 Pillars Approach ensures that side of the equation gets equal time going forward.

CHAPTER 11

Control Expenses and Add Efficiencies

I'm the first to admit that my least favorite thing is hiring and staffing! That's why I focused on training pretty quickly and wanted to make it more efficient and even better for the business. I learned that if I set new hire expectations early by spending more time intensely training up front, before they ever work the floor, employees are either going to be more successful or quickly realize that this job is not for them. I now use a dedicated part-time training manager to keep it really consistent and it helps me hold people accountable because I know they were shown the right way to do things.

Shannon Kemp

Winston-Salem and Greensboro, North Carolina Style Encore franchisee since 2014 Style Encore is a division of Winmark Corporation

When I bought my second store, I realized I needed to start doing some things differently because I didn't want to spend more time working in the back of the business when I needed to be in the front growing the business. I made some changes to save us time and money such as using an external payroll company and finding marketing opportunities that covered both stores. Later, when Shannon bought Style Encore, we were able to spread the costs across both brands.

Mike Kemp

Winston-Salem and Greensboro, North Carolina Play It Again Sports franchisee since 2003 Store employee and then manager in the franchises before he purchased in 2003 and 2008. Play It Again Sports is a division of Winmark Corporation

One might think expense management is basic Business 101, meaning most of us would understand the importance and make it part of our monthly accounting. I took it in school and teach it to freshman students and now confess to you that I was tempted to overlook it—and often did. Until, that is, I had a lean year and learned what I had been missing. When it comes to making money, the equation is pretty simple: Revenue minus expenses equals profit. It's the expense part we focus on in this chapter.

Too often, eager franchisees do what most entrepreneurs do: pay a lot of attention to how much money is coming in the door, and very little attention to controlling what's going out. Increasing your profits is not only about gaining new clients, raising prices, and adding new products or services. Your profits can grow when you generate zero new revenue dollars by controlling your expenses. Add increased revenue to your equation and you just dramatically increased your paycheck.

We'll start by developing your baseline metric for three of the most common heavyweight expenses in franchising: compensation, maintenance and overhead, and food costs. (I include food costs because, according to a study for the International Franchise Association Franchise Education and Research Foundation published in January 2017, approximately half of all franchises involve some type of food service, not including others, such as eldercare and childcare, which have large food expenses). The other two large categories, rent or mortgage and franchise royalties, are not included because they are considered to be fixed costs.

For each of these expense categories, we'll apply two expense reduction strategies: strategic cost-cutting and strategic efficiency increases. By the end of the chapter, you will have a total of six different ways to decrease your expense percentages in order to increase your profit.

Compensation

This is the big one for almost every business—franchise or otherwise—and it can be complicated to dissect, but I recommend doing exactly that in order to thoroughly comprehend (Level 2) what you are dealing with before targeting anything for reduction. (I suggest an easy way to do this later in the chapter).

Included in compensation are many separate costs, such as wages, benefits, workers' compensation insurance, administration fees, and payroll taxes. Some franchisees outsource all or parts of these, including the administration.

Eric Holm owns 31 (and counting) Golden Corral franchises in Florida and Georgia. He outsources certain human resource functions because he found it to be a "cost savings tactic and the best way to ensure compliance with fast-changing regulations and requirements." Eric has been awarded franchisee of the year nine times. The man knows what he is doing. You'll hear from Eric in **Chapter 14: This Is How You Sleep at Night**.

Others, frequently when starting out, use an employee leasing company and may later move to outsourcing the payroll only. Leasing companies in general provide a very valuable service allowing us to spend more time focused on our business instead of trying to be HR specialists. Understand, though, you may be giving up some control and you may not be aware of some of the embedded costs associated with outsourcing that add up to increased expenses. With leasing, your payroll processing costs, workers' compensation, and benefits are sometimes rolled into one big weekly or bi-weekly cash deduction. A detailed report from your processing company will break down the totals. Then you can ask questions. You need to know exactly what you are paying for because you may not need it, want it, or be taking full advantage of it.

Before you start analyzing and comparing your overall compensation expenses, break out workers' compensation insurance and benefits. The rest of the associated costs, such as processing and taxes, should remain. Here is a quick review of why these two compensation components need a completely thorough review and how you can use that information to cut compensation expenses.

Workers' Compensation Insurance

Workers' compensation insurance is a required and costly expense I watched very closely because it can be lowered with diligence and attention to detail. Talk to a workers' comp insurance representative to better understand this profit drainer. Ask questions including all available employment categories for your segment and how your employees, and you, are currently categorized. Not all employees should have the same, usually high, category code.

Leasing companies generally pool clients—which, in effect, fixes your workers' compensation rate at an average even if you have experienced very few claims and might be entitled to a lower rate if you were not in a pool. Conversely, if you have a high rating, employee leasing may be a cost-cutting strategy. I experienced both of those scenarios until I learned and decided it was time to take more control by contracting with a workers' comp carrier. I kept my rating and payments low by consistently emphasizing workplace safety and rewarded the entire team with an outing or party the years we met maintained our rating.

If you go this route, make sure you have a good agent who is committed to helping you receive the lowest rate possible and will coach you through the claims process. I once had a case open for 18 months that ended with a positive resolution and a healthy employee back-to-work that could have blown up and been a worst-case-scenario were it not for good counsel and some hand-holding along the way.

Employee Benefits Programs

Employee benefits make up the compensation expense I recommend watching and managing very closely. Most franchisees want to be considered caring people, especially in the beginning when we are wooing employees—and providing benefits helps. It also reduces turnover if you are hiring the right people, who need and want benefits and internally promote your benefits program.

Work with a benefits consulting company to help sort out your options and maximize your compensation dollars. If you are leasing employees, you'll be able to compare this to the rate you currently pay. If you do offer benefits, be prepared to get and stay involved or it will cost you more than the face value of the policy. Each month, someone needs to ensure you don't overpay, primarily because turnover requires administration, communication, and follow-through in order to make sure you're properly credited for employment changes.

I provided benefits throughout my ownership and changed up the plans from time to time. By changed up, I mean cut back when I needed to. No shame.

Wages and Administration

Now that you have examined the compensation expense, you are ready to look at it through the lens of the 3 Levels of Knowing:

- **Level 1 – Perception**: Record monthly, quarterly, and annual compensation amounts in real dollars and as a percentage of revenue.
- **Level 2 – Comprehension**: Compare your compensation metrics to your franchisor's numbers, your system's top performing franchisees, and an industry number outside of your system. This will likely reveal a few surprises, some good and some bad. Bad equates to opportunities for you to decrease expenses and increase profits.
- **Level 3 – Projection**: Format and record the data for short-term goal setting and long-term planning. (The more information you have, the better the 4 Pillars Approach works, and this approaching is for your long-term success.) Then set a realistic reduction goal for this year. If you are below the norm, you may want to consider raising compensation wages or adding other benefits, especially if turnover is an issue you want to address.

Now let's look at what to do with those numbers.

Strategic Cost-Cutting

There are many ways to cut wages. The less-strategic are to reduce payroll hours across the board, lower the starting hourly wage, and decrease your staff. Sometimes one or even all three of these are required when you have to make a big difference fast. Applying wage reductions strategically is a different matter. A good place to start would be to find out how TPFs in your system control this cost and see what would work well in your business.

In childcare, the franchisor number and industry metric was 50 percent for compensation as a percentage of revenue. I ran at about 42 percent and generally paid a higher starting wage and a much higher management and administration salary than any franchisee I was aware of in my system. I achieved this without cutting staff or hours across the board by regularly evaluating the traffic flow and adjusting the weekly schedules before they were distributed.

How many times have you walked into a retail establishment and seen too many employees standing around for the foot traffic that day? It happened to me recently when I went to a big box pet supply to get a few necessities for my four-legged roommates. All I could think of was that horrible flushing sound as the profits for the day went down the drain and I wondered, almost out loud, who was in charge. It was all I could do to not offer a complimentary business consultation. Instead, I found the elder-kitty litter and old dog pill pockets and left.

Most franchise environments are very dynamic. A built-in process for weekly spot checks of your schedule is the best way to approach this strategically. Have a well-communicated plan and policy for slow days. They are part of running your business, and whoever is in charge of that shift is responsible. They start with "Who wants to go home early?" and then go to "Whose turn is it to go home early?" if no one wants to leave. There are other ways to do this, of course; just have a plan and get people off your clock when they are not needed. Many students, mothers, fathers, and others are happy to gain a few hours of personal time. Have a list ready for your Manager on Duty to go down when he or she finds the business overstaffed on any given day.

Strategic Efficiency Increases

A hidden cost of wages is the resources it takes to find the right people to staff your franchise. Turnover in franchising is a fact of life and can run as high as 70 percent in some food service segments. In a 2011 *Franchising World* article, I read about Harold Jackson, a multi-unit franchise owner in the Great Lakes area. In the article, Jackson outlines several strategies for combating turnover, none of which are outside the realm of your capability or budget. He estimated the hidden cost of replacing an employee is between $700 and $1,000, but that's not even the full picture. We all know clients notice a revolving door and that turnover socks employee morale right in the gut.

When you develop your metrics for wages, take the time to determine your turnover rate and compare it to those of your industry, your franchisor number, and the TPFs in your franchise system. Then do some math and, using $850 as an average, determine how much profit is going out the door when employees leave. Get serious about tackling this metric and put a program in place to specifically address it. Building Layers of Loyalty and using assessments are a good place to start. Jackson recommends assessments at all levels to ensure the right people are in the right position. He realized a significant percentage decrease in turnover and expense cost when he incorporated assessments consistently. You can read the full article at www.franchise.org/strategies-to-combat-employee-turnover.

Depending on your business cycle, you may find that streamlining your hiring process is another way to strategically increase efficiency and decrease compensation expenses. Rather than piecemeal hiring, we generally tried to have two job fairs a year to stock up our candidate pool. It didn't always mean we had the perfect people at exactly the time we needed them, but it forced us to create a professional and thorough process for interviewing and screening, and it decreased the number of panic hiring situations, which almost never turn out well. Additionally, a surprise synergy occurs when you have a job fair. Your current staff members up their game when they know you have a ready pool of applicants.

Maintenance and Overhead

This category is a gold mine for cost cutting and increasing efficiencies. Consider starting with some of your least-sexy but higher-dollar recurring expenses, such as janitorial and utilities, and work down from there.

Because this category can and usually does encompass a lot, I recommend you make an executive decision here and pick only one or two expenses you think can be reduced if you focus on it. Then get to know your numbers. (This process should sound familiar.)

- **Level 1 – Perception**: Record monthly, quarterly, and annual expense amounts in real dollars and as a percentage of revenue.
- **Level 2 – Comprehension**: Compare your percentages to your franchisor's numbers, your system TPFs' numbers, and an industry number outside of your system.

- **Level 3 – Projection**: Set your realistic reduction goal for this year and create your format for tracking these throughout the year. Sketch out what you are going to do, including a time frame, to get this expense decreased and then dedicate the time and do it.

Use this newly created format for tackling one or two other expenses over the coming year. Limit it to what will not take you away from other Pillars or impede your enjoyment of your business. This is a balancing act. There is always next year, and there will be more metrics to guide you when you get there.

Strategic Cost-Cutting

This category requires you to take a hard look to "spot" the profit drainers. (You'll get my intended pun soon enough.) Many franchisees overlook it for that very reason. Therefore, before I share my personal best for strategic cost cutting in this category, I offer this good old-fashioned parable for your consideration:

One of my new friends, Tim Bradbury, a European Wax Center franchisee, gave me this gem for thinking about strategically controlling expenses. "An older entrepreneur friend of mine pulled me aside after a workout one day and shared a story his grandparent told him. He said, 'Don't take your eye off the mice. Most people focus on the big elephant in the room and how to get that high-cost elephant to move out, but they don't notice the five mice in the walls nibbling away at their profits. Next thing you know, those five mice turn into 500 mice and they've been eroding profits for a long time. Keep your eye on the mice in your walls.'" Tim adds, "We now talk about going on 'mouse hunts' and everyone knows immediately that we're looking for the small, incremental cost savings to increase profits."

I love these stories that help remind us of something so obvious that can make a difference. I'm glad Tim took time to listen to his wise friend and that he shared that with me for you.

Now let's talk about an example of "spotting" the profit drainers. Keeping carpets and vinyl tile clean in a large childcare center is a very big job, and it was an expense that dogged me for years. I tried doing it in-house as well as using different companies over the years. You know from your experience at home, the quality varies and so does the pricing, and the two do not always correlate.

I finally cut the cost to an acceptable number by taking a strategic approach: Spot-clean (there it is, punned again) every six weeks; full-clean the next six weeks. Yep, it was as simple as that. The carpets stayed fresh and clean and I reduced my cost by 25 percent, which equated to several thousand dollars a year. I also realized I needed to teach and preach. I taught the staff how to quickly tackle spills that would otherwise result in a nasty stain, and I preached that every thousand dollars I spent on keeping the carpets clean was a thousand dollars I did not have to spend on raises and benefits. I meant it and they got it.

End of story. It worked perfectly well once I found the right company that was willing to put together an annual contract which worked for my business. After that, we put a similar approach in place for vinyl tile, saving several thousand more dollars a year. And *that* is the other important aspect of this example. Find the right company, even it takes years, and the savings will come.

Strategic Efficiency Increases

Without knowing more about your particular franchise, I can't specifically advise you on how to run your operation or order your supplies more efficiently. But I do know this: Efficiencies and cost savings come when we streamline processes, especially the process of contract renewals for services, supplies, maintenance, and overhead expenses.

As a franchise owner, sharpening your focus to deal with expenses and vendors requires a particular state of mind that can be difficult to maintain. Some days, you may even have an avoidance strategy in place. It's the same kind of thing that happens in our personal lives. The last thing you want to do is pick up the phone and have a chat with your cell phone or Internet provider about your annual contract. So, you don't do it until it becomes absolutely necessary to correct an error or change something, and you find out you could've been saving money all along.

If you employ that same no-strategy strategy with your franchise, you will no doubt experience decreased profits. Over time, your profits will shrink little by little as your vendors and contractors raise their prices each year.

It's easy to implement a plan that puts the control and the profit in your hands. I recommend picking one month each year to review, evaluate, and negotiate your service, supplies, and vendor contracts. You should look at anything that involves maintenance and overhead expenses. Then contact each vendor and specify that you have a time frame to meet and are willing to look at paying quarterly instead of monthly in exchange for reductions (if you are). Ask them to look at what additional services can be provided for the same amount or what decreases could be expected in exchange for your loyalty this year.

Do what you need to do to get it as favorable as possible for the expense decrease you are seeking, and then put it away for a year. Done. Money saved and interruptions minimized. Your productivity increases and so do your profits. Another synergy that comes from this is that your staff can tell any inquiring prospective vendor you review contracts in the month you designated and that vendor should contact you the prior month.

Food Costs

Many franchise systems have absolutely nothing to do with food. They cut hair, prepare taxes, or sell tires. If your franchise has absolutely nothing to do with food whatsoever, I'll hold out hope that you can apply a portion of this information, perhaps on stealing and loss prevention, to another similarly controllable expense.

We learned earlier in this chapter, approximately 50 percent of franchised businesses have some sort of food costs as an expense. For a franchised hotel, it could be a pure expense item as it is in eldercare and childcare, where for others, it could be a matter of controlling how much of the profits your employees eat, steal, or both. For many of our franchise brethren, it is the whole enchilada—their profit center, plus the eating and "friendly" giveaways, which is why it made my Big 3.

Use the same three-step process to get to know your food costs as you did with your compensation and overhead and maintenance metrics:

- **Level 1 – Perception**: Pare down your food expense category to arrive at a base number that can be used for comparison purposes. Determine the percentage of revenue you spent on this expense last year.
- **Level 2 – Comprehension**: Compare this food cost percentage to the numbers from your franchisor, TPFs, and your industry.
- **Level 3 – Projection**: Format it in a way you can use going forward for annual planning, draw some conclusions, set a realistic reduction goal for this year, and sketch out a plan of attack.

Strategic Cost-Cutting

Franchises in the restaurant or retail food segment usually have very specific requirements for sourcing. Therefore, the following strategies are general suggestions intended only for sourcing those items or groups that have not been addressed explicitly or implicitly by your franchisor.

The information in this section was provided by my longtime high school friend Brian Bone. Brian has owned two very reputable and successful produce sourcing and delivery companies for more than 30 years. His current company, Vine Ripe, is a highly sought supplier for many of the independent full-service restaurants in Central Florida, including several at the Walt Disney World® theme parks. These are Brian's suggestions:

- **Increase delivery frequency.** Frequent deliveries should mean super-fresh product that is ready to use and serve, which increases food yield and decreases waste due to food spoilage.
- **Limit vendors.** Using a small selection of vendors instead of spreading out your purchases among many will allow you to increase your purchasing power by buying in greater quantities and should bring a lower price point to your invoices.
- **Check every invoice.** Checking item by item ensures all credits are applied and that the quantities received are the quantities billed.
- **Review pricing.** Reviewing food costs regularly will keep your vendors from notching up the prices, which they do, and remind them you have options, which you do.

And here is another tip, this one provided by me:

- **Balance food quality.** You can save money by providing some less-expensive staples people want along with some signature items you want them to have and that they will notice and appreciate.

That proved to be a challenge until I made a surprising discovery. As a childcare owner, I worked hard to introduce healthy, less-processed food into the monthly menu rotation. My goal included having a variety of foods some children may not eat at home, including meatloaf and chicken enchiladas. To the best of my ability, I balanced these more costly but healthier menus with more traditional, low-cost chicken nuggets (all white meat!) and PB&J sandwiches (on whole wheat!). It was frustrating because I could not achieve the metric I wanted with my new healthier menu.

Then I learned the reason. It happened on Meatloaf Day. Between you and me, I don't care for meatloaf, but what I learned that day was that my staff apparently craved it. I had returned earlier than expected from an appointment and walked straight into the children's cafeteria. To my surprise, no one was able to greet me with the usual "Hi Miss Christy!" because, you guessed it, they were too busy eating to notice me. Even using the "spork" utensils, their mouths were full of meatloaf. Truthfully, it was pretty hilarious. The ducking and turning that ensued when they spied me in the room could have gone viral on You Tube. It took me a few moments to realize what was going on, but once I did, I addressed it immediately. The new policy (which was clearly posted) became this: "Staff members are welcome to enjoy a child's-size meal portion as long as they are sitting and dining with their class."

It wasn't long after that revelation that my food metric fell in line and the healthy menu stayed. I introduced my healthy meal and snack menu as a true competitive advantage strategy. For many clients, it was highly valued.

Examine your food costs carefully, ask questions, and observe. The strategic part is finding ways to lower this metric without hurting food quality and having clients (or staff) go hungry.

Strategic Efficiency Increases

Owning and running a restaurant is not for the faint of heart. The more research I conducted, the more respect I gained for those involved in the food industry. I'm going off the grid a bit here, because I would be doing a disservice to you if I did not focus on employee thefts, so I am addressing them here as a Strategic Efficiency cost-cutting measure. You'll soon understand why.

I found some helpful information in a webinar from LP Innovations of Milford, Massachusetts, a firm that provides loss prevention solutions focused on earnings improvement. The webinar quoted a 2004 report by the National Restaurant Association that showed theft represents on average four percent of a restaurant's total food costs. You know your numbers and can do the math.

The following are some of the highlights from the webinar titled "Restaurant Theft and the Hard Truth About Losses in the Food Industry."

- **Where theft occurs:** throughout the business, among servers and wait staff; bartenders and bar staff; chefs, cooks and kitchen staff; back-office employees; management; operators; and vendors.
- **What they steal:** food and products; cash including out of registers; deposits and receipt manipulation; meals and giveaways; credit card numbers; kitchenware and supplies; and intellectual property including concepts, recipes, and trade secrets.
- **How they steal:** self-imposed breaks; the short ring, where the customer pays a higher price than is rung into the register; "free" food and drink; phony walk-outs; voids after closeout; and register skimming. These examples are from "8 Ways Your Staff Is Stealing from Your Restaurant Right Now," an article by Kendal Austin posted on the Toast Restaurant Management Blog.

What LP Innovations recommends for theft prevention:

- Incorporate a theft prevention program. A developed program will better protect your business. If your franchisor is silent on this, go to external resources.

- Involve your staff through education, training, and awareness about theft prevention. I wish I had done that.
- Investigate and resolve issues involving theft promptly, and understand it can happen at any time.
- Seek more knowledge about theft prevention.

If your franchisor does not have this on the agenda for the next owners conference, be the one who asks for it. Now that you are aware of this ugly truth, help increase awareness and learn together how to keep employees from stealing your profits.

It's Basic: Common Sense

Controlling expenses isn't always strategic in nature. Often it comes down to basic common sense, as I discovered in my business.

Utilities and the way we control them can be grounds for divorce. You know what I'm talking about. One person leaves the lights on, even when he or she leaves the room and the other one turns them off even when someone is sitting there with a book open. One person huddles in sweatshirts and blankets and the other is sweating with the fan on and the thermostat set to 68 degrees. Having this utility battle at your franchise is similar, but oh so much costlier in terms of your profits.

At my childcare center, all the thermostats were controlled in the main office. When I say "all," I mean eight different thermostats controlling 13 different classrooms in the Main Center and four thermostats for five classrooms in the Enrichment Center. Besides the teaching staff having different body types and varying in ages and stages from pregnancy to menopause, they also had to deal with the building architecture, placement of the classrooms, and time-of-day temperature fluctuations.

Maintaining a comfortable air temperature throughout a twelve-hour day and two shifts of (mostly female) employees was extremely challenging. But we tried. At least I did. I'm the one who saw and paid the mid two-thousand-dollar power bill each month. Remember, we were in Florida and that amount was consistent year-round. This expense was always on my target list to control. Or rather, *try* to.

I was a venerable maniac about cleaning and replacing air filters, opening windows when it finally cooled off, and even turning up the air-conditioner earlier in the day during certain times of year. I was strategically trying to control this big overhead cost.

Then one fine day, during my "walk-about," I made another surprising discovery. I saw several classroom doors leading to the playgrounds propped wide open. I don't know exactly when it started, or how long it had been allowed to continue, but apparently door-propping had become the standard for controlling air temperature. Finally, it all made sense. No wonder my cost-cutting strategies hadn't been working. Once I realized door-propping had become pervasive, I nipped it in the bud. I'll never forget the sheepish looks I got that summer as I did my rounds and asked the offenders, "Would you do this at your home?!" That seemed to curtail the door-propping, at least when I was there. Magically, that expense metric came down and my profits increased.

That big fat mouse Tim Bradbury talked about earlier? *Gone.*

Strategically controlling expenses is clearly not one of the "fun" parts of owning a franchise, nor was this one of the easier chapters to write, but I did it—*for you.* Finding ways to make more money is pretty great. So, schedule the time it is going to take, and set your sights on how much profit you are going to add to your bottom line this year. Multi-brand, multi-unit franchisee, Shirin Kanji, points directly to efficiency when asked about his business philosophy for a Franchising.com article. "Efficiency is doing things right," he says. "Effectiveness is doing the right things right." Make strategically controlling costs and finding effective efficiencies part of your business philosophy.

Speaking of profits, it's time to address the other half of the profit equation: revenue. Let's Mine Your Metrics for Revenue Gold and increase your profit even more this year.

CHAPTER 12

Mine Your Metrics
for Revenue Gold

Don't make the numbers too complicated or fragmented. Use a few key metrics and focus on behaviors that drive reasonable, yet challenging goals and then reward great job performance by having large rewards and recognition. The people in the organization will take charge of their own work to move the business forward without ownership constantly telling them what to do and how to do it. Be a coach and a cheerleader, not a dictator!

Ruth Ann Grimsley

Kansas City, Kansas
25-year Great Clips multi-unit franchisee
19 salons in Joplin-Pittsburg, Kansas City, and Springfield, Missouri
Began career with Great Clips in 1982, became a franchisee in 1993

With expenses under control, or at least *on notice*, most franchise owners will feel more capable and motivated to get down to the business of building a revenue plan. This chapter is about *the other half of the profit equation:* increasing revenue that, when combined with cost-cutting and efficiencies, leads to you being a more profitable franchisee each year.

When it comes to increasing profits, revenue by far gets the most attention. And, why shouldn't it? Calculating revenue involves easy math that points to a straightforward increase in profit. But there is more to it than that, especially if you incorporate the 4 Pillars Approach.

Increase Profit *and* Margins by Increasing Revenue

Once your business is established, and you have data you can rely on and experience under your belt, business principles dictate that growing your revenue will increase your profit *and* your profit margins. The primary reasons are efficiencies and predictability. You get better at running your business and your staff gets better at working there. A business can handle more sales, more clients, and more output without an equal increase in the expense ratio if the business is run well and your market remains constant.

Because markets are not 100 percent predictable, the 4 Pillars Approach helps you exert the needed control internally and externally to respond to fluctuations. With the 4 Pillars balanced, maintained, and getting higher, look out: Here comes the profit. Your profit will grow as you increase revenue, and your margins will grow to the highest optimum level for your franchise. That's where the 20 percent and the TPFs reside. That's your business Sweet Spot.

If you try to haphazardly grow your revenue, without doing the work behind the scenes on the 4 Pillars, your business won't realize margin growth to its full potential. You will also miss out on the 4 Pillars synergies that make your life and your business better. You might even get frustrated and give up. If you find and choose ways to grow your revenue as part of a cohesive plan for the year, one that is in sync with your franchisor and the 4 Pillars, you will achieve maximum financial benefits and the complete professional satisfaction that comes from creating a growing business on a firm foundation.

Bottom line is this: Working your franchisor programs with the 4 Pillars Approach will lead to increased profit margins in addition to increased profits. Here's the plan:

- First – We mine and establish goals.
- Second – We develop specific programs to achieve the goals.
- Third – We design and announce a reward program to ensure success.

In order to mine, we have to get back to basics. This is where the payoff comes.

Know Your Revenue Metrics

At the risk of being accused of beating a dead horse, we're going to talk about knowing your metrics *again*. Not because I'm trying to fill pages in a book, but because it's *that* important. I *really* want you to get this. If the only thing you remember from this book is the 3 Levels of Knowing and how they apply to your numbers, that alone will make a huge impact on your business. The specific steps for growing your revenue are (you guessed it):

- **Level 1 – Perception**: Develop a monthly and quarterly baseline for your revenue for your last full year. Optional – If applicable, include a monthly breakdown of specific revenue sources. Record your profit as a percent of revenue alongside the monthly and quarterly revenue numbers and then for the full year. When you spot a month that reveals a higher or lower revenue, take a closer look. Break down the weeks and see what's there. This will take some time. It's supposed to. This is how you begin building your important Money Metric Pillar, and you need the full picture to increase your profitability and your overall profit. This data will become invaluable.

- **Level 2 – Comprehension**: Compare your annual revenue and profit numbers against your franchisor's metrics (the information you paid for when you bought a franchise) and those of your TPFs. One time, just so you know, go outside your system for a similar brand or talk to a non-franchise business owner with a similar business. All you need is figures for annual revenue, and profit margin. You want to know, beyond a doubt, how you compare. Mine and dig for more information within your data. Digging often leads to discovery and new insights for revenue growth that are pure gold.

- **Level 3 – Projection**: Record and format the data for short-term goal setting and long-term planning. Then stop.

Step One: Mine and Establish Goals

Armed with your revenue metrics, franchisor program notes and any surveys, comments, and ideas you've been saving, start by reviewing the past year. The purpose of the review is to mine all that data for revenue-building gold. Look for anomalies and patterns such as a month that showed a revenue spike.

For instance, upon digging, you learn (or remember) an elder care complex brought a bus full of residents to your painting studio on Tuesdays last February. Should you market to other similar businesses this year? That would be an easy yes. Or let's say you noticed a higher profit margin in July this year as compared to last year even though the revenue was the same. You mined and see that your manager was on vacation for 10 days and your assistant manager held a contest to see who could sell the most product at your personal services franchise. Those are exactly the kinds of nuggets you are looking for.

Next, you turned to the current year franchisor programs and had to admit, even though you didn't emphasize the new programs as much as you could have, they added to the overall revenue in spite of your complacency. Should you refresh and relaunch this program or wait for the next program to be introduced and commit to it in earnest this time? Yes, and yes! Do both.

Looking back, with actual data, will almost always yield ideas for future revenue growth. Your first pass at this should reveal some choice nuggets. Write them down. If nothing jumps out, don't worry. Sometimes metric reviews need to percolate before you go back with fresh eyes. In the meantime, I'm going to give you a few revenue-building ideas to help stimulate your thinking. There are many others and you should use your best judgment when deciding what should be discussed with your franchisor representative before implementing. Over the years, I found my franchise representative to be a great sounding board for revenue-building ideas and programs. I'll expand on the first three (A, B, and C) to help you get started.

Start by Identifying Your Best Mining Opportunities

    A. Windfall Opportunities (for new client revenue)

    B. Franchisor programs (incorporate new and existing)

    C. Bundling or packages (services or products)

D. Incremental sales (add-ons and promotions)
E. Target vertical markets (first-time or return promotion)
F. Performance goals
G. Expansion (existing location or buy a second or third unit)
H. Other

Try to suspend judgment and be open to any thoughts and ideas as you read through the remainder of the chapter. Take your time and take note of anything that comes to mind. Think of this as your highly focused brainstorming session, and *anything* goes when you brainstorm.

A. Windfall Opportunities

Windfalls can lead you to new markets, new ways to market, or a new large and profitable client. Windfalls in business are unexpected revenue gains you do not cause, or control. Windfall opportunities can be developed when you pursue more information that leads to new and sustainable sources of additional revenue. For example:

- Did your catering business show promise in a new vertical market as evidenced by a big order delivered to a medical office? What was the revenue impact? How can you leverage this knowledge?

- Did your sign, printing, or consulting franchise see a spike one month because the local university decided to subcontract some of its work during a crunch? What was the revenue impact? What other departments at the university could you approach? What other colleges are in your area?

- Was there a valuable new client who was referred by someone who might be in a position to refer you similar clients, such as a real estate agent or rental management company? What was the revenue impact of that client? How can you leverage this information? Should you approach other real estate agents and management companies and ask for their referrals?

My Windfall Example

Over the years, there were many windfall opportunities with my business. This one stands out.

As you know, I mingled with clients when the time was right. One month, I focused on a specific topic and asked about their career and workplace. I learned that three or four of my Sweet Spot Clients worked for the same defense subcontractor. Armed with that information and the knowledge that these were very satisfied customers, I contacted the company's human resources department and offered an ongoing promotion for their employees and their families. It was a win-win. Soon we applied this same promotion offer to other area large employers with good success.

WINDFALL OPPORTUNITIES EXERCISE

Brainstorm and write down three to five windfalls you experienced in the past two years. Circle the two that have the best opportunity for increasing windfall revenue this year.

1. _____
2. _____
3. _____
4. _____
5. _____

B. Franchisor Programs

Did your franchisor introduce any new programs this year that you have not yet fully incorporated? Did the franchisor share any "reveals" of products, services, or campaigns at the owner's conference that will be introduced this year? One of your biggest potentials for growth is to incorporate all franchisor programs and marketing campaigns. Who can you target that will be excited by the introduction and inclusion of franchisor programs? Ask fellow franchisees what they did or call your franchisor representative if you come up empty-handed.

My Franchisor Program Example

In the early childhood education segment, service is important, but what you teach the children and how you do it carries a lot of weight. Over the years, my franchisor produced increasingly sophisticated curriculum that directly benefited the children's education. I was grateful for this. However, it wasn't until I attended a workshop at an owners conference and listened to the remarks of other owners that I realized I was not taking full advantage of how comprehensive it was or the support materials to promote it. When I got back, I arranged the front office to highlight our emphasis on curriculum and revamped our pitch when someone called in to inquire about our services as well as our center tour talk for prospective parents. I also under-utilized summer camp promotional materials until I mined and saw an increase in camp revenue when I took full advantage of what was available.

FRANCHISOR PROGRAM EXERCISE

Write down your top-of-mind ideas for better incorporation of franchisor programs. Circle two that have the best opportunity for increasing franchisor program-driven revenue this year.

_____

_____

_____

_____

_____

C. Bundling or Packaging

Here are a few questions to stimulate your thinking: What do your clients like the most about your business? What is your lowest-revenue service, product, or time of day? Which holidays or special occasion days are coming up? Which client (profile) buys the most or least of what you sell? What resources do you have that are currently underutilized?

My Bundling or Packaging Example

Managers get very creative when they need incremental revenue to hit a bonus target. One that stands out involved punch cards.

For a limited time, clients with school-age children could buy a 10-day drop-in punch card at a discounted rate that could be used throughout the year. The savings equaled approximately 15 percent or $50. It was incremental revenue because there was never a guarantee that we would get their drop-in business when the public school was closed. This helped ensure we did and, for me, the operational cost savings of collecting money one time instead of in 10 small transactions covered the discount. This program was so popular we ran it two or three times a year, turning that incremental revenue into a regular promotion that guaranteed a good month when we needed it. Many franchises have incorporated similar frequency buying programs that build client loyalty and add incremental revenue. I say, bravo! It definitely worked for me and works on me when it's offered.

BUNDLING OR PACKAGING EXERCISE

Based on the questions above, brainstorm ideas for bundling or packaging existing products or services. Remember, *no judgment.* Circle two that have the best opportunity for incremental revenue this year.

_____

_____

_____

_____

This step is complete when you have established financial goals for each of the revenue-increasing ideas you commit to this year. I suggest approximately two to four per year as long as they do not all run concurrently. List them in the program chart below and record your revenue goal for each of your programs.

Step Two: Design and Announce a Reward Program to Ensure Success

Over the years, I had cash bonuses, gift cards, and even a spa weekend for achieving an annual "stretch goal" to keep the team focused and motivated. I recommend small rewards for achievements relating to weekly or monthly goals and a quarterly, bi-annual, or annual goal with larger incentives and rewards.

Here are two examples that demonstrate this point very well.

Scott Kallen, a seven-year Philly Pretzel Factory franchisee in Pittsburgh, PA, does periodic $50 spiffs to keep his team focused on the daily sales numbers when he thinks they need the extra motivation. The simplicity, immediate rewards, and instant public recognition work very well for his franchise. His revenues increase substantially every year. You'll hear from Scott in **Chapter 15: Planning Your Profits**.

Other Top Performing Franchisees, like multi-unit Great Clips owner Ruth Ann Grimsley, design programs that focus on performance goals over a longer period. This year, her salon managers and a few other lucky team members have an opportunity to win an all-expenses-paid cruise. Here's how Ruth Ann explained their Get on the Boat incentive:

"Every salon manager who hits the two specific salon goals for a six-month period is getting on the boat. In addition, we've set two measurable, individual performance-driven goals for the salon team members. Every month of the contest, the team members who meet their individual goals are entered into a drawing for a chance to win and join the group of managers cruising." Ruth Ann said all the team members who achieve the goals will be recognized in a meaningful way, even if their names aren't drawn.

What's clear is that these two franchisees know how to use metrics and rewards to motivate individuals and teams, and to drive performance and revenue that leads to higher profits. They are both good cheerleaders *and* great coaches.

REWARD PROGRAM EXERCISE

Brainstorm a few small incentives and larger rewards for achieving performance and revenue goals. If you are new at this, don't overstep your comfort level. Folks like Ruth Ann have had years of experience, and she would be the first to tell you that your employees will appreciate whatever you do. You will make adjustments along the way as your business needs and budget dictate. Be sure to mix it up and include some *fun*.

Small Incentive Awards	Larger Achievement Rewards

Step 3: Develop Specific Programs to Achieve the Revenue Goals

Most programs will be able to follow a Who, What, When, How, and How Much format. Now complete the chart (using the prior exercises and your most recent notes and ideas) to the best of your ability. This tool should be used to organize your (incremental) revenue programs in a way that gives you an overview of your plan for the year. Make it work for your franchise and adjust or change it as needed.

REVENUE GOALS EXERCISE

Revenue Source (Mines)	Who (Target)	What (Action)	When (Time Frame)	How (Specifics)	How Much (Revenue Increase)	Investment / Reward (Cost to Implement & Reward
A. Windfalls						
B. Franchisor Programs						
C. Bundling or Packaging						
D. Incremental Sales						
E. Target Demographics						
F. Performance Goals						

Use this chart as a guide for your planning and review and adjust it periodically as you organize and formalize your annual plan for growing a stronger business this year by increasing your revenue.

Most franchisees, strike that; most *business* owners do not know their Money Metrics, including expenses and revenue numbers to the extent you now do. Use this knowledge. It's powerful for controlling your profit numbers, including your margins. Done on an annual basis, your long-term success is almost ensured. *Almost.*

There is one more factor that has the potential to diminish your profits. But don't worry, in the next chapter, I'll show you how to ensure the franchise you bought last year, or 10 years ago, continues to be the business of choice for your existing and prospective clients. That means, making sure your franchise is and remains *truly* competitive.

CHAPTER 13

If You Build It, They Will Come…But Will They Keep Coming Back?

One of the things that keeps me so competitive is to consider the possibility of failure. Fear of failure is my competition. If I fail, then my customer will not come back. The little things that are important to the customer are the easiest to do, but being truly innovative like adding a glass installation division within my business, getting approved partnerships with major national insurance companies to provide collision repairs, and the integration of online parts ordering are just a few examples. For me, finding ways to improve the customer experience is what is what leads to increased profits. That's what you have to incorporate into your business to become truly successful.

Brian Greenley

Littleton, Colorado
Maaco franchisee since 1990
Owner of the #1 franchise of Maaco
Maaco is a division of Driven Brands

W hy is it so important to be competitive? What does that actually mean? You may think your clients "like you" and so aren't overly concerned about your competition. Or maybe it's just not your nature to think competitively. If not, it's time to make a shift, because you *need to be competitive.* My job is to help you gain a fresh, real-world perspective on being competitive and learn why it's important you make this a systematic part of your job.

I want to help you to stay one step and at least one year ahead of your competitors *for the duration of your ownership.* Over time, I think you will find this to be one of the more enjoyable parts of your job. I know I did and based on my interview with Brian Greenley, and many other top performing franchisees I interviewed, they enjoy it too. I'll tell you more about how Maaco, led by Driven Brands President, Jose Costa, aggressively achieves their sales goals, but first, I want to make certain you have an appropriate competitive mindset.

Why is Being Competitive So Important?

My favorite way to frame the importance of being competitive in your business is to recall the iconic 1989 baseball movie *Field of Dreams* and the often-repeated line "If you build it, they will come." (This is actually paraphrased from two quotes in the movie: one by the character played by James Earl Jones to the lead character played by Kevin Costner, "People will come, Ray," and another by a mysterious voice that repeats, "If you build it, he will come.") The concept refers to Costner's character's desire to reunite the eight Chicago Black Sox players who were accused of intentionally losing the 1919 World Series, and he wants to do that by building a baseball field in the middle of his Iowa cornfield. With your franchise, "If you build it, they will come; *but will they keep coming back?*" sets the appropriate tone for being competitive.

In the beginning of your franchise tenure, you may be the only game in town. With certainty, that will not last. That was my experience when I opened in 1998. Over the years, I became the bulls-eye as more than a dozen new centers opened all around me. Many of them are still very successful, reputable brands and franchise operations. I had to learn how to be a tough competitor. I had no choice. It was about survival. You know what I went through to get there, and I wasn't about to give that up. I decided it was better, and more fun, to be competitive strategically than worry about another new competitor opening in *my* market.

"If you build it, they will come" was my mantra throughout the loan, build-out, and pre-opening phases of my franchise, with more than a few prayers thrown in as well. If I build my dream franchise, clients will come. I bet you had a similar version of this that kept you going when the going got rough.

Congratulations! You Built It, and They Came

And so did the competition. Now what?

If you have someone like Driven Brands President Jose Costa at the helm, you are among the more fortunate. Jose, who was featured on the TV show "Undercover Boss" in 2015, is not shy about how he views positioning his company by changing the current landscape in order to achieve success. Jose spoke to me about how "working closely with a large group of 50 franchise owners helps ensure the Maaco brand moves in the right direction. Together, we test new services and then collaborate."

He explained that this model has worked to expand services across retail consumers and gain additional commercial fleet clients and currently is being piloted to offer same-day collision repair services. Those closest to the local market, the franchise owners, help shape the competitive strategies and ensure all owners have opportunities to grow their revenue and profits.

In my book, *that's* being competitive and a strategy I can get behind.

For me, one really big takeaway from our conversation was that Jose recognized his franchisees know what will work best because they know their local market better than the corporate office. In this chapter, we outline how to build a True Competitive Advantage strategy that works for you and your local market.

This is extremely important. Your revenue projections depend on your ability to be truly competitive.

Make Sure They Keep Coming Back

I learned, as you have, that it's not enough to *get* clients. You have to keep them coming back. As consumers, our natural inclination is try what is "new and pretty." Who doesn't like to walk into a brand-new gym or yogurt shop? When you first opened your business, you were the "new and pretty" in town.

It's only a matter of time before a copycat competitor opens down the street, does a direct mail campaign targeting your key demographic, and takes over part of your revenue. Your important Level 3 Money Metric revenue projections depend on your ability to be competitive.

Think of it this way: Level 1 and 2 Money Metrics knowledge represent the current state of your business and what has happened in the *past*. When you project *future* growth, Level 3, you might incorrectly assume your market remains in steady state and that nothing will change. This is not realistic. It *will* change, and competitors will want your clients or your clients will want to try something different. Your job, as a strategic leader, is to prevent this from happening.

If you build and maintain a true competitive advantage with your business and strengthen your position by adding layers of competitive programs over the years, then yes, they absolutely will keep coming back and remain for years. Otherwise, the answer is a lukewarm "They might," and might is not going to get you into the top tier or ensure you meet your revenue goals for the year.

This chapter focuses exclusively on how you build a true competitive advantage into your business. The astute reader might ask, "I thought the Loyalty Pillar was going to make sure they never leave? Why now do I need to worry about the competition?" The answer is that the 4 Pillars work together to Strengthen, Protect, and Grow your business. They all play an important role and complement each other. Maintaining a true competitive advantage provides additional assurance that firmly puts you in control of your business and therefore your success. You've come too far to take any chances.

Another, equally astute reader might say, "It's the franchisor's job to make sure our brand is competitive." I understand that position, to a point. However, that only gets you halfway there. I strongly urge you to consider it your job, after the honeymoon period is over and your business is established, to hone your competitive instincts and implement strategies that will keep your business relevant in your local market. Your franchisor's job is to keep your brand strong and viable. Only you can keep your clients from straying and your revenue growing when your market heats up. And it's never too late to start.

Don't worry, I'll keep it straightforward. You keep reading and taking notes. This may be the missing piece that ties all your hard work together and helps you become that successful franchise we are both picturing.

COMPETITIVE INVENTORY EXERCISE

Many business people have the wrong idea about what constitutes a *true* competitive advantage. This quick exercise will help you identify and develop your true competitive advantage.

List three to five qualities, elements, or features that make your business competitive.

1. _____
2. _____
3. _____
4. _____
5. _____

Characteristics of a *True* Competitive Advantage

Now check your list against these three core characteristics of a true competitive advantage. (I'll explain these in more detail later in the chapter.) Only one characteristic needs to apply for an item on your list to be deemed a true competitive advantage.

- Your franchise has qualities, features, or elements that are **hard to duplicate** *and add value for your clients.*
- Your franchise has qualities, features, or elements that require a substantial amount of **time and ingenuity** to incorporate *and add value for your clients.*
- Your franchise has qualities, features, or elements that position your business to be **distinctive in your (local) market** *and add value for your clients.*

I'm (still) a betting woman, and I'll bet two out of the three on your list do not meet these characteristics. If I'm wrong, that's great news for you. This chapter will help you keep it that way. If I'm right, your business may not be as strong and secure as you think it is, especially when your market starts to heat up. Either way, you can solidify your true competitive advantage by being able to clearly articulate how and why your business is better than those of your competitors. This will help ensure your business continues to grow even when "new and pretty" comes to town.

Developing a true competitive advantage takes time and starts with a brutally honest assessment of your business strengths with this new way of thinking. Let's review and examine each of the three core characteristics and some strategies you can implement now to help you develop them.

Characteristic #1: Hard to Duplicate

This strategy dictates that you have allocated resources of time, energy, and/or finances that your competition has not and the end result is widely valued by your clients. It does not mean the competition will not or cannot do or offer something very similar. Generally, the more unique and valued, the higher the price you can command. And the longer you can hold this uniqueness position, the more valuable it is to you. Ideally, by the time your competitor duplicates your strategy, you have another one in place.

Strategy: Location

High-dollar examples include buying or leasing a unique piece of real estate such as a terrific corner lot or the ideal location in a popular shopping center. With these examples, you have effectively taken that competitive move off the table for your competitors.

Many franchisors sell several units at a time in one general geographic area for this specific reason: It creates total market coverage, a true competitive advantage that is hard to duplicate. As a customer of a popular sandwich franchise, you can get your favorite choice anywhere you go in town. Same with personal services, fitness franchises, and many other brands.

Location is such a big advantage that some franchisees use sheer force of will and perseverance in lieu of making uncomfortably big real estate investments. Securing permitting when the odds are stacked against you is what BurgerFi did in my hometown of Winter Park, Florida. It was the first, and years later remains the only, franchised restaurant on posh Park Avenue. I used this strategy when I expanded into the new planned community of Avalon Park. I wasn't willing to build a standalone building and so outmaneuvered my competitors by figuring out how to fulfill the challenging playground requirement with a leased space configuration. The expansion maintained the Hard to Duplicate advantage in that community for more than two years, which was enough time for me to establish a loyal client base before a competitor opened nearby with a freestanding building.

Strategy: Consistent Change

I found this example in the December 2015 issue of *Franchise Times*. Mathew Corrin is CEO of Freshii, a fast-growing fast casual franchise that targets Millennial customers. He combs the country for healthy, trendy, and unique foods as he goes about his daily business supporting owners and growing new franchises. He changes the menu on a regular basis, every 70 days, which keeps his Millennial clients intrigued, engaged, and coming back for more. Certainly, other franchisors *could* adopt this Hard to Duplicate strategy. Doing it successfully is a different matter. The degree of difficulty is high enough that most don't, and certainly not to the degree Corrin has done keeping Freshii's competitive advantage firmly intact.

Strategy: Key Relationships and Marketing Programs

A rock-solid relationship with a Sweet Spot Community Partner does double time as a competitive strategy. When you are noticing unique partnerships over the next several weeks and contemplating who to approach, I recommend looking for ones that, in addition to helping you bring in revenue, have the potential for building a Hard to Duplicate competitive advantage.

Here's an example: Because the target market for our services was busy working families who dine out frequently, we developed a simple, low-cost effective layer to our marketing program that turned into a true competitive advantage. Each month, an employee on our marketing team dropped off small promotional boxes of crayons with fun and educational coloring sheets highlighting our curriculum theme for that month to local full-service restaurants that also catered to this demographic.

The combination of consistency, including meeting the child's expectation of something new each month they dined, and the service we provided to the restaurant, made it hard for our competitors to duplicate our strategy. Even competitors that were much closer to the restaurants could not edge in on our cheap and effective marketing program. The restaurant owners were very loyal to us, and our staff and clients often received discount dining coupons from the savvier ones.

Characteristic #2: Time and Ingenuity

There are many opportunities for you to impress your clients and add value, but a true competitive advantage should meet the minimum threshold of one year. In other words, for the advantage to be legitimate and worth your time and effort, it should take your competitor at least that long to catch on and implement a similar advantage. Generally, the more time and ingenuity a strategy takes, the longer it will hold as an advantage. This strategy is not typically costly. Instead, it's the ingenuity involved that keeps your competitors from doing it first.

To help build your creative confidence, consider these ideas as potential areas for building your next true competitive advantage.

Strategy: Technology

Is there a simpler or more convenient way to pay or track invoices online? If you own a business services franchise, whether your primary revenue is driven by B2B or B2C, there are many opportunities to help clients assimilate and consolidate their year-end planning and pre-plan for the next year. If you own a travel services franchise, perhaps there is way to help clients or companies plan and budget for their next trip?

One business services franchisee I interviewed, Jeff Mackey, who owns a successful Pillar To Post Home Inspectors franchise, bought iPads for his team of inspectors before they were so prevalent. His strategy was to increase response time for the younger-trending homeowner who expects instantaneous reporting and the Realtor partners who also value that quick response time. Think of something involving technology that would add value for your clients and is not being provided by your competition.

Strategy: Education

In the early childhood education field, a child development associate (CDA) certification is an important differentiator for quality of staff. Teachers with CDAs have better classroom management skills leading to well-run classrooms with happy children. Happy children beget happy parents. With the goal of having a 100 percent CDA-certified staff, I arranged for instructors from the local community college to teach the CDA curriculum in-house for one year. This included two evenings a week and occasional weekends. I paid the tuition and testing costs for everyone who participated. Travel time and the frustration of registering were now non-issues. I was delighted by the enthusiasm and the team spirit and, almost as an afterthought, invited other Kids 'R' Kids owners to include their staff.

It was a huge success. Upon completion, all teachers received a well-deserved raise and the self-satisfaction and confidence that come from a meaningful achievement. The end result was that we were the only school in the area that had 100% CDA credentialed teachers. This, while being meaningful to my staff and me, could have been a big "so what?" if it were not for one thing.

I publicized this goal to parents before we started, throughout the year, and after the coursework was completed in order to emphasize and reinforce the value they would personally derive. Parents appreciated the employees' commitment to the children and their profession and my commitment to the employees. From that point forward, we did not hire anyone without a CDA or a Teaching Certificate and maintained this true competitive advantage long-term.

Strategy: Client Incentives and Rewards

These can come in the form of a loyalty program, pricing program, partnership, or some type of add-on or extra benefit. Please do not let this catchall term restrict or limit your thinking. The goal is to offer your clients something they will remember, brag about, and see as a value that your competitors cannot or will not offer this year.

We developed a client loyalty program that included complimentary Parents' Night Out (PNO) coupons and extra vacation weeks. While some parents used the PNO coupons the first weekend they got them, others never did. Or the vacation weeks. Still, because the idea of a free Parents' Night Out was catchy and fun, we always shared this loyalty program tidbit in the tours we gave to prospective parents.

Characteristic #3: Distinctive in Your Market

Making your *brand* distinctive is largely the franchisor's role. Making your *business* distinctive in your local market is *your* responsibility. Many consumers still think of franchise locations as part of a national chain or a large corporate entity. We have to work smarter to be considered a local small business in our buy-local small business economy.

Your franchisor probably has several great suggestions already spelled out and ready to roll out if you inquire and research. You might be pleasantly surprised by the enthusiasm and the information you will receive when you ask for help and ideas.

The four categories I used to incorporate distinction into my franchise were being socially responsible, sharing my story, being first, and developing a unique service program.

Strategy: Social Responsibility

Social entrepreneurism is a growing theme in America's business climate, and the franchise industry has caught the wave with the Giving Back theme and veterans franchise programs. It's not only good, it's good business. As a conduit for "good" in the community, you show that you care and are here for reasons other than making money. If Millennials are a significant part of your client base, or you want them to be, then this is even more important for you. Social entrepreneurs get a fair share of their discretionary dollars, and they will seek out businesses that give back. Research also shows that they are extremely brand loyal, so help them find you.

Start by researching organizations that have a mission that resonates with your clients and matches your passion. In other words, be strategic. The best choice would be one that has a natural tie to your business. Don't rush this decision. Think of the long-term relationship that could develop. Do your homework. The best organization would be one that has an excellent reputation, has a willingness to educate you and your staff, and has a good social media presence.

Some franchisors and franchisees create their own "give-back" instead of aligning with an existing organization. Remember Eddie Titen from **Chapter 4: Connect with Your Community**, the Sonny's BBQ franchise owner in Tampa, Florida? His brand stands out in a very large and competitive market. He and his franchisor created their unique BBQ To The Rescue community program, and in addition to doing good work in their respective communities, it's a competitive home run for those franchisees who make this a priority.

If you choose well, plan well, and are consistent with your activities, a social responsibility or give-back program that makes you distinctive in your market can work as a *long-term* true competitive advantage.

The synergies are numerous, including improved teamwork, renewed employee motivation, and increased exposure to potential new clients.

Strategy: Share Your Story

Blake Mycoskie, the founder of TOMS, highlights the power of sharing your story in his social entrepreneur's guide book *Start Something That Matters*. He recounts the time he was standing in the security line at Los Angeles International Airport and noticed that a young lady in front of him was wearing a pair of TOMS shoes. He commented, "Cool shoes!" To his amazement, she exuberantly shared the entire company story and ended with a pitch directing him to go buy a pair. Those Millennials I mentioned earlier? I *know* they want to hear your story, and others need to hear it, too. Mycoskie's book is required reading in my class. (That was only one of the great tips you can pick up from reading this short book that will give you insight into how Millennials think and what makes them tick.)

Your story is as unique and important to your clients as your franchisor's story was to you when you opened. Try thinking about it in this way: You fly your brand flag at the top of the pole, but yours could be flying right under it. Sharing your personal story with your clients makes you more a more authentic local small business owner and approachable. When people "know you," they are more committed and supportive of your business. Those people include your employees and others you want to attract, not just your clients.

I recently read a Franchising.com article about the origins of family-run Impact Properties. (You met Shirin Kanji in **Chapter 10: Know Your Numbers**.) Impact Properties currently has revenues of more than $60 million annually, yet Shirin's father started the company living very humbly with his family in a small apartment before buying his first hotel property in Gainesville, Florida. If I were a franchisor awarding territories or a convention planner needing a large block of rooms, I wouldn't hesitate to do business with Impact knowing what I know now.

That's the kind of story that draws people in, like loyal employees and franchisors. Perhaps try to reveal your story in an article you write or a profile for an award you receive and post it in your lobby and on your website. Pictures also work really well. I displayed a collage in the area where prospective clients gathered information showing "how it all started," our community engagement, and the various (good, bad, and awful!) hairstyles I sported over the years.

Strategy: Be First and Be Original

Being first at something your clients value is the purest form of a true competitive advantage. It shouts, "leader in your field" and shows your clients and prospects you intend to stay on top. Being first to install Internet cameras in my center was one of the best ways to jump-start my business. It was expensive and it was not required by the franchise owner at that time. As usual, Pat Vinson, my franchisor, was right; it was well worth the expense. The publicity that came with it was priceless. Once I was given that "gift" of being first in the city, I never hesitated to be first again.

Strategy: Unique Service Program

There are many ways you can define and develop this. Many of our best ideas were adopted from other businesses and industries. (No shame in borrowing.) Here's a quick one to stimulate your thinking. We offered complimentary notary service for our clients. It cost me about $150 a year to keep the notary status active for one or two key staff members. We needed this to run our business efficiently anyway. We mentioned it in a very offhand way during our tours to prospective families. They loved it *and* used it.

No-brainer.

Who is Responsible—You or Your Franchisor?

Before you make firm strategic plans that are outside of the bounds of the current operations manual, I highly recommend clarifying your understanding of where the line of competitive responsibility lies between you and your franchisor. If you enjoy a good relationship with your franchisor, you may be the franchisee who gets permission to try something new.

I had lunch with multi-unit fast casual franchisee who opened a location a quarter-mile from a very large university campus. He and his investment partners are sometimes asked to take on troubled locations, which tells me he had developed a strong loyalty relationship with his franchisor. He shared that he was contemplating a discussion with his franchisor to allow a discount meal program for college students. This successful franchisee clearly knows where the line is and wasn't going to cross it for short-term gain.

If you are unclear about where the "line" is and don't have real access to your franchisor, there are many other ways to develop an aptitude for knowing. Consider joining a franchisee online discussion group or contacting your franchise relations committee (FRC) or franchise advisory committee (FAC) representative. Your quality assurance or other franchisor representative is a more direct resource. I found it was helpful to use all resources available. If you have remaining questions, send an email to the president or call the CEO asking for clarification. The longer you own your franchise, the easier these things will be to discern.

Under the Radar?

Perhaps your idea is a one-off and you just want to try it without a lot of discussion. Understandable. Sometimes, forgiveness in lieu of permission is OK, but use it sparingly, even if you have a good relationship and your royalties are paid on time and paid up. Like any relationship, if you are doing your fair share of sharing, the better the likelihood of getting a green light on a new idea or forgiveness for an idea already implemented—especially if it is showing real results. Generally, the better your relationship is with your franchisor, the more open the door will be for testing your ideas and suggestions to ace the competition.

Balance your desire to do the right thing in the right way with the knowledge that your franchisor wants you to run your franchise like an owner, and that includes—within guidelines, of course—doing whatever it takes to get your fair share of your market *and then some*. Yours is a partnership and your responsibility to that partnership and to your family is to increase your business.

Getting Started

The more you focus on and engage in honing your competitive advantage, the more effortless and enjoyable this part of your ownership will become. Here are some tips to get you started:

- **Write it down.** Keep an ideas journal or e-notebook with you at all times. Start noticing what other businesses do to set themselves apart. What do you respond to? Capture any thoughts, no matter how "offbeat" they seem; they can be developed later and often turn into something very useful. If you notice you're lacking entries in your journal, try getting out more to see what your competitors and others are doing.
- **Take stock.** Ask yourself, "What would absolutely propel my business this year? What do our clients ask for that we don't do, and why don't we?" Review the reasons why clients (especially Sweet Spot Clients) left your business and why others come. You may be missing something obvious. If you don't know the answers, give them a call and ask questions.

- **Borrow heavily.** Borrow ideas from the more successful franchisees in your network and comb your franchisor resources for old campaigns and other things that may stimulate competitive strategy thinking. You may find some buried treasure to polish and reframe that you forgot about. Reading industry publications like *Franchising World* and attending conferences are also great places to listen and learn, especially from Top Performing Franchisees. They know what works. Find one and develop a rapport.

- **Involve the team.** Add this topic to your next staff meeting agenda. Your journaled notes should be used to kick off a brainstorming session. Some ideas will be no-brainers (let's do this!) and some will be non-starters. Others, however, will be ripe for development and may turn into a longstanding true competitive advantage. Very soon, you and your team will become skilled competitive advantage scouts with abundant ideas for future layers.

- **Cultivate feedback.** Conduct a client survey. Done right, this can provide a wealth of information and generate some new ideas. Practice "Yes, and…" as in "Yes, that's an interesting idea, and we might also …" with clients and staff to show you are really listening and keep the conversation going when someone has an idea.

- **Do what you can do.** Do not get hung up thinking you need several strategies every year. Not too little and not too much for *your* business, *this* year is the right amount. Your objective is to define competitive strategies that make a difference and implement changes of quality. Not quantity.

- **Communicate.** Share your program with your clients before you roll out your plan and again when it starts and again upon completion. I did this when the Enrichment Center was green-lighted to keep clients from straying to a "new and pretty" competitor. Always stress the benefits the client will receive.

- **Delegate.** You may find that one team member really shines and takes ownership of this process. Consider giving that person a leadership role and a small raise. This "Competitive Liaison" position is creating someone's valued career development in addition to creating valuable white space for yourself to work on your business away from distractions.

And last, is there a movie or song that inspires you when you need a "Rocky" inspirational moment? I led with my "If you build it" mantra to keep me from becoming complacent. What's yours? No need to brainstorm this one. You'll know it when you hear it and you can't get it out of your head. (Just don't forget to write it down!)

Building Pillar 3 is one of the most challenging, maybe even *the* most challenging, aspect of franchise ownership. Having goals and planning the programs to consistently support them is what gets and keeps you in the top tier and firmly in control of your business.

Method Management, the final Pillar, is a "how to" to help you put this all together and strategically *focus* on your business so you don't get derailed. You've come much too far to let that happen.

Pillar 4

METHOD MANAGEMENT

Focus Your Business

Question: What is the *one* thing top-tier franchisees do differently that sets them apart from all the others?

Answer: They are *relentlessly focused* on their business.

Those owners who consistently and seemingly effortlessly reside in the upper echelon of your franchise system do not compromise when it comes to their discipline and ability to do what needs to be done—and that requires focusing on their business. Specifically, on the things we've talked about. *How* they focus is what keeps them there.

I purposefully placed Method Management, the focus pillar, at the end of the book because, frankly, it's the toughest to get through and I didn't want to lose you before you got here. It's also the tough love part of the book. Method Management requires an honest assessment of how you run your business *now* and a commitment to do the work and then to hold yourself accountable. Self-accountability can be the hardest part of franchise ownership, but with the 4 Pillars Approach, it's built into your business and your plan.

If the first three pillars represent what you do to Strengthen, Protect, and Grow your business, then Method Management is the "how you do it" pillar. Specifically, it's the structure and framework for putting your annual plan together, and build balanced pillars, one successful year at a time. Method Management is not a new business term. You may even want to call it something else as you become more entrenched. Just know that without a framework and a methodology to keep your business on track *and in balance*, the odds of getting the results you want are greatly decreased.

This final section begins with an explanation of the tools you use to build and implement. You've been reading about them throughout the book and now I'll explain how and why they work together.

Method Management is what will take your franchise into the next tier and the one after that until you are at the very top. *And then it will keep you there.* The next thing you know, you are the franchisee making it look effortless with increased time and energy to focus on the things you enjoy most about your business.

Your strong 4th Pillar takes you right where you want to be each year. Now, let's get focused!

CHAPTER 14

This Is How You Sleep at Night

What keeps me up at night? Things that are difficult to control. In the food business, that means food safety and also what the one-percenters might say on social media outlets. So I stay focused on building careers, not just giving someone a job, because loyal employees breed loyal customers. At least a third of my managers came out of the crew.

Eric Holm
Winter Park, Florida
Golden Corral franchisee since 1996
Multi-unit owner with 31 restaurants in
Orlando, Florida, and Atlanta, Georgia
Nine-time Franchisee of the Year winner

know you're smart; probably a lot smarter than me, but that doesn't mean you don't struggle to stay on top of all the functions of your business that are ultimately your responsibility. I know I struggled. That's why I had to create a framework that allowed me to conceptualize, communicate, and, most importantly, *execute* my planning for the year. Method Management became the way I built and tracked ideas for growth, which led to increased revenues and profits almost every year I was an owner. After I discovered what Method Management could do for my business, I slept like a baby. *Even during economic downturns.*

When I started writing this book, I contemplated for days how to explain Method Management as the way you put together everything we've talked about, the Layers of Loyalty, Strategic Leadership, and Money Metrics. And then it hit me: Think of Method Management as your instruction guide or blueprint for building the pillars. Having a guide helps you avoid major missteps while you're continuously improving your business.

Even savvy franchisors find that decision-making using a common framework ensures the business is aligned. For Jacksonville, Florida-based Brightway Insurance, the brainchild of founders David and Michael Miller, that framework was an Operating Mandate that reflects their personal values.

Very simply, it is W-cubed, or Win-Win-Win. "Everything we do must be a win for our Agency Owners, a win for customers and a win for Brightway," David Miller says. "If it's not a win for all of the stakeholders, we either figure out a way to make it a win or we don't do it." Looking at business decisions with that lens ensures Brightway's interests are completely aligned with their franchisees', or, as David says, "we measure our success in only one way: by our franchisees' success." Win-Win-Win is a sturdy framework. You need one equally as strong.

Like David Miller, your franchisor did not intend to address every single aspect of your business, including your unique local market, when you were awarded a franchise. Your franchisor wants you to run your business to the very best of your ability while staying within the scope of the franchise agreement. In order to stay focused, 4 Pillars franchisees concentrate on short-term goals. Your long-term goals are securely fixed in the back of your mind, but it's the short-term plan, using Method Management to guide you, that gets and keeps your full attention.

Short-Term Focus for Long-Term Results

Method Management focuses almost exclusively on short-term goals—what needs to happen *this* year to propel your business forward. It may sound a bit counterintuitive, but when I stopped worrying about the future, my head was clear and I became more energized and more productive.

I'm not the only one who thinks this way. S. Truett Cathy, the founder of Chick-fil-A, revealed his short-term thinking philosophy in the 2007 book *How*

Did You Do It, Truett? His son, Dan Cathy, is quoted as saying: "Dad chafes at the idea of thinking more than six to eight months in advance. Dad doesn't plan long term because he likes to take advantage of unexpected opportunities." He goes on to explain the other benefits of thinking short-term, including "the ability to zero in on what's most important for the organization in a given year, and with short-term focus, he has the time and resources to do that."

In "The Right Location" chapter, the founder tells of being the first "quick meal restaurant" in Atlanta's first enclosed shopping mall in 1967 as an example—even though it was a hard sell to convince the mall developer that it would work. It was a great early example of short-term thinking serving him well. Mr. Cathy was able to jump on an opportunity because he didn't stay stuck in the here and now and didn't worry about five years in the future. It wasn't until mall development was slowing down in the mid-1980s that the first standalone Chick-fil-A was built. At that time, there were 330 restaurants in malls. You know the rest of the story.

Still privately held and family owned, Chick-fil-A has steadily grown every year since the famous sandwich was developed in 1967. The company now has more than 2,200 locations, and it reported nearly $8 billion in revenue in 2016 with the highest average sales per store in the industry. That's a strong testament to the power of how having a short-term perspective releases you to focus on the most important objectives and allows for flexibility in order to respond to opportunities and market conditions.

From this point on, if you commit to align your business to the 4 Pillars Approach, your focus must be on having a successful franchise *this year*.

This is How You Do It: Three Basic Tools

With Method Management, there are three basic tools for implementing your plans: processes, programs, and layers. These tools are the "how-to" for systematically and efficiently incorporating the other three pillars into your organization. **Programs** are what create the changes you have targeted. **Processes** are how you implement and execute the programs. You build your Loyalty, Leadership, and Metrics Pillars with **Layers**, or layering.

Let's look at how you can use each of these tools to build the 4 Pillars Approach into your franchise.

1. Programs

Throughout the book, I've shared many programs from my own business and from others that may translate well to your business. Some of mine were developed when my business needed something completely new to further drive revenue or snuff out a competitor, while others complemented an existing program my franchisor had in place. Method Management gives you a systematic way to first determine what your business needs based on your goals for the year, and then to address those needs by creating new programs, renewing or refreshing existing programs, and omitting those that didn't get the results you were seeking.

2. Processes

In my experience, the top-tier franchisees are generally very process-driven business owners. A business process is a set of defined tasks performed to accomplish a specific objective or goal. Processes enable business generalists, like us, to successfully implement, manage, and create change in our organization. A well-developed process will increase the success of your program.

Your franchisor has built many processes into your operation to provide order and consistency of product quality, service, and delivery, among other things. Method Management processes will either complement an existing franchisor process or will be designed by you when you need a new set of defined tasks to drive a program.

3. Layers

Many business owners too often do nothing because making a change is too daunting or overwhelming. Making changes is easy with layering. On an annual basis, layers are added or removed depending on the needs of the business and the success of existing programs. Layers are used to build your 4 Pillars Approach by placing new programs on top of existing programs. The layers are strategically added, refreshed, or deleted each year, as needed, to keep your business strong, protected, and growing. Layering is a powerful, strategic tool that gives you the ability to try new things and a way to make adjustments as your business dictates.

Franchisees who use the 4 Pillars Approach are successful entrepreneurs because they control their business by fine-tuning processes, programs, and layers in direct response to or anticipation of market conditions. Method Management with a short-term focus gives you the framework, responsiveness, and flexibility to navigate the terrain and control your business.

To Complement or to Create?

Before further explaining and refining how to use these essential tools, it is important to understand and distinguish when complementing an existing franchisor process is the best approach or when creating a new process is a better course of action.

Here are two examples that highlight the difference.

Complementing an Existing (Franchise) Process

Many franchises have staff positions that require licenses, certifications, or continuing education (CE) hours. These are time-consuming, annoying, and difficult to keep up with, even with the franchise software management system. Better to have a process in place that can address all of these in a way that maximizes productivity and efficiency for your franchise. At Kids 'R' Kids, we had a state licensing requirement for annual CPR and CE hours for all staff. The first few years, we chased employees down until they showed proof of completion. It was awful. With a Method Management mindset, we implemented a process that quickly turned this into a "business as usual" task, saving countless hours each year and decreased the annoyance factor to nearly zero.

Two Saturdays a year, we brought in a CPR-certified trainer and made attendance of one a requirement of employment, which employees acknowledged in writing in their files. It didn't matter that your CPR card didn't expire for three months, it was required if yours expired before the next training. In one afternoon, files were updated and completed for six months. Staff members saved time and money by not having to find and pay for a course on their own and were paid a two-hour training wage. (Yes, you can do that.) We implemented similar processes for our bus drivers, who have numerous requirements including annual physicals. The documentation efficiencies were so dramatic that we incorporated CE time for a portion of each staff meeting and looked for other areas we could streamline using this process. We found many.

Your franchise may not be as documentation-oriented, but there are other areas of your business, such as employee reviews or facility maintenance inspections and documentation, that could be much less aggravating, time-consuming, and costly with a new or complementing process. Freeing up managers and others to focus on more important things, like increasing client loyalty and building revenue, requires creating more efficiencies in your business. Better processes help you do that.

Before you begin building your 4 Pillars Approach, I recommend a review of your current operation to identify what needs immediate attention in your franchise. Whatever takes more time than it should, pulls your managers away from more important things, or bugs the heck out of you is a good place to start. Think about what is not getting done consistently, on time, or to your standards. Functional areas of your business, such as hiring, reporting, cleaning, and scheduling need to run very efficiently before you start building your 4 Pillars Approach in earnest.

EXISTING PROCESS EXERCISE

Identify three areas that need immediate attention and therefore an improved process.

_____

_____

_____

Creating a New (Franchisee) Process

New processes are different and are usually based on the new programs you want to introduce this year. I'll share an example now, but don't get discouraged if it's not crystal clear after this first pass; it will be by the end of this chapter.

When it comes to developing a new process to drive a new program successfully, you'll first need to outline the scope. State the goal and then the details and parameters needed to implement and drive a program for the first year. For example, if you want to add a **marketing program** to build your revenue and Money Metrics Pillar, you may decide that a marketing team would be the best way. Creating a process that implements and sustains a marketing team would look something like this:

Question: What is the goal?
Answer: To increase awareness, bring in new clients, and increase revenue.

Question: Who will do the marketing?
Answer: A small team of existing staff.

Question: How many hours a month would be budgeted?
Answer: Approximately 15 hours per month total.

Question: Who would be a good fit and is friendly, professional, and ready for something new?
Answer: Full- and part-time staff members who know the business, are friendly, are professional, and have my trust.

Question: Can your managers provide staffing coverage for them while they are marketing?
Answer: Yes, in two-hour blocks. On Tuesday through Thursday the schedule can be adjusted to allow one marketing shift per week during their normal schedule. Any events scheduled during non-business hours will be posted in a communications binder for sign-up, with two marketers per event.

Question: How will they be paid?
Answer: In their regular checks. They will be on the clock when they are marketing. After-hour events will be compensated with a separate check and a separate marketing wage (yes, you can do this) to be paid on the Monday

after the event. Immediate compensation keeps them motivated. (Cash is king but you didn't hear that from me.)

I met with the targeted employees to review the team requirements, set a time for team training to go over scheduling, communication responsibilities, and expectations. Schedule a quarterly or biannual meeting in advance, establish goals and define how they report their activities. A simple marketing and communication binder works well for keeping details organized and the team on track.

A team approach works well for keeping motivation high and generating ideas, but the process needs to be as seamless as possible or communication gets muddled quickly. For example, I suggest including having an extra person "in the wings" for emergencies, vacations, and absences. This substitute position can be used as a "try-out" for joining the team. Throughout the design and implementation, be prepared to make similar adjustments.

With that, your marketing team is officially launched with a process in place to sustain it. *Done.*

Now you can focus on the program details that will attract new clients who strengthen, protect, and grow your business *this* year.

Before You Act

You know what I'm going to say here.

Before you implement a major new process, you should check in with your franchise representative. Your representative knows *things* and might steer you to another franchisee who has developed something that is working well, or steer you away from something that did not work. Sometimes the issue I was working on was going to be addressed in a software update or other franchisor initiative and I could get the same, or better results by waiting a few months. One five-minute phone call to check in with your franchisor may help you avoid unnecessary frustration down the road and definitely will help build your franchisor Loyalty Pillar. (Synergy!) while you effectually tackle something else.

Method Management Example

A good employee loyalty program leads to more-dedicated employees who stick around (this year). A good competitive program keeps your clients from leaving (this year) and a good Go Big Leadership Program shows your community you care (this year) and attracts new clients who stay long term.

The objective of any new program, or variation of an existing program, should be to help you achieve your specific goals *this year*. In the following example, two goals are incorporated demonstrating how Method Management layers, programs and processes can be streamlined for addressing more than one goal at a time and how synergies occur throughout your operation when you implement the 4 Pillars Approach.

Goal: Decrease Staff Turnover and Increase Customer Satisfaction

If you want to decrease turnover by recognizing employees for excellent customer service you would design a program that would focus on the Loyalty Pillar.

First Layer

You decide to add a Merit Awards **program** and use it to target excellent customer service. This is a loyalty pillar **layer**. Employees can trade in their merits for paid time off (PTO) or gift cards, which leads to increased employee loyalty and better customer service. The program has specific details you have outlined and announced at the beginning of the year, but it will not be truly successful until you have designed and implemented a **process** to track the merits, the rewards, recognized the recipients publicly, and promoted it *consistently*.

New Process

The process outlines the specific details of the tasks required to implement the program, including who does what, when, and how to ensure the program runs seamlessly. You know a program is a hit and your process is solid when you hear staff members bragging about their awards and your managers are executing flawlessly. If you heard employees grumbling that the time off was difficult to schedule or that managers didn't have desirable gift cards to award then your process needs attention. Either too many PTO hours were awarded (because you made it too easy) or the back office needs to tighten up the execution of the awards before the program loses momentum. You have effectively built up the Loyalty Pillar and strengthened your business with better customer service when grumbling been replaced by smiles and clients extend compliments for their recent exceptional service experience at your establishment.

Next year, you may decide to target something else with your Merit Awards program because the process worked so well and you now know it would be a cinch to add another loyalty layer. (And the fact that some of the compliments were posted on social media didn't hurt either.) With the 4 Pillars Approach, you know the metrics and your current market conditions will help you make that decision *next year*.

Enhancing a Layer

Using the same loyalty example, awarding employees PTO for excellent customer service with your Merit Awards program is one layer. At the end of the year, you look at your turnover metrics and client satisfaction survey and know it was successful and well worth the investment. You wonder if expanding this would further decrease turnover and consider other ways your team members can earn merits. If you decide to add awards for, scheduling flexibility or excellent attendance this would be considered a program *enhancement*. Changing up a popular existing program by making it a deeper layer is a quick "yes, let's do it" and much easier than starting something new.

If you find the turnover number remains unchanged and fewer awards are issued the following year, you might conclude that the Merit Awards Program was no longer having an impact and take that layer completely off the Loyalty Pillar. (Yes, you can do that.) As long as it is communicated well in advance and you don't pull up in a new BMW the next day, it will be fine. Especially if you communicate something new is "coming soon."

Second Layer

Your business is growing, you feel more confident, and you believe this is the right time to tackle the turnover problem once and for all. You decide to add four paid holidays as a benefit, and a replacement layer for the Loyalty Pillar is now in place. (I paid six holidays: four hours for part-timers and eight hours for those who worked full time). As a strategic leader, adding paid holidays is a Go Big Employee Leadership move that you now know, should be the move that gets you where you want to be. *Done.* Next!

Method Management Creates Synergies

Layering will create synergies between the Pillars—often with very little or sometimes even no effort on your part.

For example, you decide to focus on building **Community Loyalty** by joining the local chamber of commerce. You actively engage at meetings and occasionally invite one marketing team member or supervisor to join you. The next year, because you have found this organization to be very beneficial for referrals, you volunteer to be on the membership committee. This adds a layer to both the **Loyalty Pillar** (for community loyalty) and the **Strategic Leadership Pillar**. The high-quality leads and referrals continue to come, and the next year you are ready to step up and become the membership chair. You have simultaneously and synergistically added layers of Community Loyalty, Strategic Leadership, and **Money Metrics** (for revenue). Don't discount the added impact to the Loyalty Pillar (for employee loyalty) that occurred when you started including your staff members to join you at the meetings and events. Four very positive impacts on your business for one strategic action. Let's keep going.

Because you know your Money Metrics, you conclude that each layer was a win-win, so you stay the course. If, however, you discover it was not, (perhaps you were spending too much time at the chamber and getting few referrals), you simply back off a layer and next year choose to forego any committee work. Or you try another organization altogether.

You will find that using this method of strategically adding and taking away layers cuts across many areas of your business and helps you plan your year with confidence. You'll be delighted by the surprising number of synergies. With time, data, and practice, you'll be able to project and track revenue increases based on the investment of the programs and layers you are adding, enhancing or subtracting.

Building and adding layers with programs and processes is an incredibly effective way to systematically strengthen, protect, and grow your business, *this year.*

Busboys, Waitresses, and Restaurant Magnates

We focused on the hardcore framework of growing a franchise in this chapter, but it's the people you meet along the way who remind us why we do what we do. Eric Holm and S. Truett Cathy have a lot in common, although Eric and Mr. Cathy's family (he passed away in 2014 at age 93) may not know it. The iconic Chick-fil-A founder liked hiring family members of his loyal employees and said he could tell if a busboy was going turn into a successful young man, or restaurant owner, by the work ethic and attitude he showed at that early stage. I couldn't help but wonder what he would have thought if he'd met Eric Holm at age 14. Eric lovingly shared how at that age he started working alongside his waitressing mother bussing tables for Sonny Tillman, founder of the original Sonny's BBQ in Gainesville, Florida. Would Cathy have recognized that this young boy would one day grow up to become the successful multi-unit restaurant franchisee that he is? I think he would have.

What's more important is that they have shared the same philosophy and heart throughout their organizations, and that passion for lifting up others continues to be a huge part of their success. Eric also shared how he admired Sonny's shiny big Cadillac and often told him so when he rode to work on his bicycle and caught up with Mr. Tillman in the parking lot. I can just picture that, can't you?

Deceptively Simple

Processes, programs, layering, and a short-term focus. That's it. Method Management is deceptively simple. Deceptive because solid execution month after month and quarter after quarter and year after year is not easy to do, and frankly, that's why many owners fall short.

Don't fall short. Commit to seeing this through because it's worth it. The Method Management framework and the 4 Pillars Approach puts an end to sleepless nights, tossing and turning, and worrying about your business. When you have a proven system in place for strengthening, protecting, and growing your business, you will sleep like a baby *every* night.

The tools we discussed in this chapter will help you to be more methodical, systematic, and disciplined with synergies that help you create a well-rounded business and the ability to enjoy the financial fruits of your labor.

Speaking of financial fruits, it's time to start planning your profits.

CHAPTER 15

Planning Your Profits

I make sure everybody is focused on the number. When you have a goal in mind and a monetary reward for your staff, why not share that? In our monthly meetings, we plan what we're going to do that month to get there. Maybe it's a party tray sales competition, it just depends. One thing is certain, though: We always make it fun. If the weather is really bad, sometimes that can be tough—unless, of course, the Steelers are in the playoffs!

Scott Kallen

Pittsburgh, Pennsylvania
Philly Pretzel Factory franchisee since 2000
Purchased second location in 2017

was not a great math student. I'm sure the last math grade I received was a C and I was glad to get it. Luckily, when I bought a franchise, I realized the math required to grow my business and make a good living wasn't really all that difficult or complicated.

Even with simple math, the tasks of setting revenue targets, cutting expenses, and planning your profits are not for the faint of heart. Or the lazy. This is where your discipline and commitment to your success can be tested. I know, because mine was tested each year when it came time to dig into the results and the reports from the current year. Don't be dissuaded by that admission. Planning your profits is one of the easiest things you can do to ensure your business grows each year—and, by far, one of the most important things you must do.

Scott Kallen, a franchisee with Philly Pretzel Factory, shared that he sets the annual revenue goal at 20 percent higher than the prior year and his lowest increase to date is a very impressive 11 percent. I'd say he is onto something. It starts with his annual plan. Let's figure out a plan that works for you.

Determine Your Time Frames

Planning your profits starts with determining time frames for planning your year and tracking your revenue goals. Most franchisors will not tell you how to set up your accounting books or structure your revenue planning. Even if they ask for your profit and loss statements, and they should, they usually leave it up to you to determine how you plan your financial year.

Keep in mind many franchisors host an annual conference or owners meeting and use that opportunity to launch important programs and share key initiatives that may impact your planning. If your franchisor rolls out new programs in June, for example, it's worth considering the possibility of lining up your planning time and even your accounting year to follow the annual conference.

The other time frame parameter is deciding how often you want to set and track your revenue goals. As the owner, you will likely want to know the weekly revenue your franchise generates, but may only share monthly revenue numbers with your key personnel because it allows for the normal monthly business cycles that most all businesses experience. There is no right or wrong.

I monitored and communicated the weekly and monthly revenue numbers, but used quarterly revenue targets because the predictable business cycles, such as summer camp, sometimes lasted several weeks and smoothed out over a full quarter. I learned, after a couple of years of ownership, that quarters worked best for my business. Do what works best for yours. You can always change it the following year.

This might help you determine whether quarterly or monthly revenue goals are right for your franchise:

Quarterly Goals	Monthly Goals
Smooth out business cycles	More cyclically bound
More time to ramp up programs	Real-time data for immediate corrections
13 weeks, including 13 Fridays*	4 or 5 Fridays, depending on the month*

Important if revenue is higher at the end of the week and if payroll is weekly or bi-weekly.

Having weekly, monthly, or quarterly revenue goals serves many purposes and creates a lot of synergies. However, by far the most important purpose of goals is to keep you and your staff focused, engaged, and motivated throughout the entire year like Scott Kallen from Philly Pretzel Factory and Ruth Ann Grimsley, the Great Clips franchisee you met in **Chapter 12: Mine Your Metrics for Revenue Gold**.

I didn't specifically ask Ruth Ann how she came up with her "Get on the Boat" awards program, but there is little doubt she knows her numbers. For starters, I'll bet she knows exactly how much additional revenue the business needs to produce and where the payroll number should be for her to feel confident she will see additional profit to cover the rewards program and pay herself for her effort.

If you aren't at Ruth Ann's level, and most franchisees are not, I recommend you start with an annual planning meeting. This worked for me for many years.

Your Annual Planning Meeting

With your time frames decided, you are ready to start planning with an annual meeting. This is a no-stress scenario which, done correctly, will increase your motivation and renew your passion for your business.

Set aside a few hours of uninterrupted time. Unless you have a partner, it's just you at this meeting, so find a time that suits you best. I almost always picked a Sunday afternoon in mid- to late November because it was quiet and I was clear-headed and well-rested. You need to be in order to focus and dig into the previous ten or eleven months of data. By not waiting until December, I gave myself a few weeks to further contemplate the targets I set. Four or five hours was enough time to ensure I had the right perspective and sketch out a few potential programs for the coming year.

If you lack the motivation to schedule your annual planning meeting, remember that intentionally and purposefully positioning your business for success, as defined by you, *this year* requires discipline, especially in the beginning. What kept me on task is the same thing that can keep you on task: The knowledge that planning your profit, not just your revenue, is the best way to ensure you will reap the financial reward you need and want as a franchisee for the coming year. Your future success and peace of mind depend on it. After the first year, I'm certain you'll agree it is well worth the investment of time.

Step 1: Take a 10,000-Foot View

Looking back on your year *before* you look forward to planning your specific revenue and profits goals is a very effective and efficient way to generate targeted programming goals to strengthen, protect, and grow your business that, done well, can create synergies across all Pillars.

I recommend you don't pick up a calculator or look at any numbers to start your review. (Yes, I'm completely serious!) It's harder to see the opportunities and answers if you start punching numbers right out of the gate. You don't want to miss anything that has the potential to increase your likelihood of success in the coming year. Instead, start by reviewing the year from a more general vantage point. Think of it as a 10,000-foot viewpoint. Ask yourself a few key questions. Did you take advantage of all franchisor programs? What revenue programs did you implement this year? Were they successful? Did any key employees leave, and if so why? Did any new competitors open in your local market? Did you have a successful leadership strategy this year?

Your goal is to gain an honest assessment of how well you strengthened, protected, and grew your business over the past 12 months and have a general outline of what you want to focus on going forward.

The most important thing is that you develop a basic system for reviewing your year and stick with it before you start detailed planning.

Step 2: Review Your Money Metrics

It's time to look at Money Metrics to see how well your programs worked financially. Now we are talking about the numbers. The objective is to gain a complete understanding of how the business performed over the past year from a financial standpoint. This knowledge will guide your program decisions for the coming year.

Start by gathering any and all reports you have for the current year. You also want to access the final annual data for the prior two to three years. The more information you have that reflects the actual financial breakdown, such as quarterly and monthly revenue numbers, the better.

Next, project your total annual revenue number for the current year and calculate your projected profit margin. Hopefully, you have a good idea ahead of time what that profit number is going to be, and certainly where you want it to be, even if your fingers are crossed. (My minimum acceptable number was 20 percent profit. Anything less meant I needed to be very cautious about adding any program expenses that didn't immediately correlate with increased revenue.)

Then look back over previous years of monthly, quarterly, and final year-end numbers and compare those with what you are doing this year. By doing this, you might notice new trends and business cycles that you would otherwise miss. It's not a science, but it's not intuitive either. Numbers will sometimes surprise you.

Here are three examples to guide you through the financial review process:

1. If you were trying to stop a trend in turnover and implemented a new vacation policy or training program this year, go back at least two years in order to see whether you successfully reversed the trend.
2. If you want to see whether the spring client loyalty program enhancement was a winner, check the spring quarterly numbers from the past two to three years to see whether it was worth the time and expense you put into it.
3. If your profit margin was low, compare your top expense items with those of the past year or two to figure out what was too high and fix it strategically.

Sometimes it's very difficult to compare numbers. You may be too new in your ownership tenure or have not been previously focused on the metrics and therefore don't have much data to compare. Don't worry, you'll get there! Generally, if you have three years of data, including your current year, you will be able to discern what is working and what is not working or is costing too much for the results you're getting.

Dig until you find the answers you need to make well-informed, metrics-based decisions, and don't give up until you are satisfied. Stick with the same perseverance you used to open your franchise. This is your money we are talking about. I have little doubt you'll soon get very good at reviewing your Money Metrics.

Step 3: Review and Plan Your Programs

This is a three-part exercise. You will need a blank piece of paper in order to complete this part.

Part 1: Create a worksheet with column headings including: Revenue Growth, Expense Control, Competition, Loyalty, Leadership, Community, Efficiency/Processes, and Franchisor Programs. (Your headings should fit your business, the way *you* think about it, but you will probably find the majority will apply to one or more of the 4 Pillars.)

Go back to your 10,000-foot view and Money Metrics review to make sure you have everything covered.

Part 2: Fill in the columns. Write down the programs you had this year that impacted that heading in any meaningful way. Some programs will apply to more than one column, and some columns will have no programs. If you added a layer enhancement, note that here. Highlight which programs worked (keep it), which didn't work (pitch it), and what needs work (enhance). Now your plan is starting to take shape. Draw a line separating this work from the bottom half of the page. This becomes a visual map that will show where you need to focus in order to strengthen, protect, and grow your business. This is your map to design in whatever manner works best for you.

Part 3: List program ideas. On the bottom half of the worksheet, under the appropriate columns, add your new program ideas for addressing the questions you asked yourself in your 10,000-foot view, your Money Metrics review, and any other notes that help you focus on what you can and need to do this year to reach your goal. Use this as a brainstorming session. Liberally include what you noted from other businesses and other franchisees. Get it all down on paper. *You are, in effect, evaluating ideas and potential new programs that will build your Pillars* based on the column headings you identified as important to your business in the coming year.

Parts 1 through 3 will take some time. It's supposed to; you are outlining a basic plan for an entire year. I recommend a break before the final step. Then, with fresh eyes, look at what you've written down before moving to Step 4.

Step 4: Plan Your Profits

Now the fun starts. Your discipline is about to pay off. You have reviewed the past year with a 10,000-foot view, conducted a thorough review of your Money Metrics, outlined the programs you ran last year, and sketched out what you want to focus on in the coming year. You know your business, what it needs, and what you can do to get it where you want it to be next year. That's exactly what being strategic is all about.

The final step is to determine what you want your profit to be next year and decide which programs and layers are going to get you there. You may want to start your planning session by delineating "best case," "most likely," and "worst case" for some or all of the calculations. This is what I call "playing with the numbers" because it's not an exact science and requires some back-and-forth calculations and a clean sheet of paper.

Based on the revenue total and profit margin you calculated in Step 2, and the revenue and profit potential of the programs you have now chosen from Step 3 (for cost cutting, increasing revenue, and squashing the competition), calculate the profit you can expect to make if you are fully committed to the 4 Pillars Approach. (Probably somewhere in between "most likely" and "best case.") Write and highlight the revenue amount you expect to generate from each of the programs and layers you are counting on. *These* are the programs and layers that will determine your success this year.

Finally, take a last look at your plan and check your math. Make a final determination what the revenue number needs to be to earn the profit-dollar amount you want your franchise to generate next year. Based on your reports and your business cycles, divide that number into quarters or months so you can see how the year looks at a glance and plan your programs accordingly. Heavy (incremental) revenue quarters need strong, rock-solid programs or you may not reach your annual profit goal. Lighter months may just need "business as usual" programs to hit the monthly number.

It's your year to plan as you see fit. The 4 Pillars Approach allows for the adjustments and flexibility you'll need as the year unfolds, so don't get too hung up on the details. You've come a very long way and should be proud. Only the best of the best know how to do this *and then, actually do it.* Congratulations. You are on your way to be among the very best.

The next step is to figure out who is going to do what and when, and face time is the best way to ensure things are going to get done. That means it's time to talk about meetings. Before you grimace, hear this: With Method Management, you can lay out the entire year with one meeting plan. Yes, seriously, one plan.

You'll learn to embrace this, too.

CHAPTER 16

Meetings Aren't Sexy, but Accountability Is

There was a time when I was working seven days, 70-plus hours a week. The fear of having to make this work was the motivator, but I pretty quickly realized that pace was not sustainable and I could lose my family and my health. It was then that I started setting boundaries and stopped trying to do it all. You either run the business or it will run you. Later that (realization) led to some major changes—including a reinvestment in my business. Now, I think about it like this: You are either growing your business or going backwards. There is no staying the same.

Jeff Mackey

Orlando, Florida
Pillar To Post Home Inspectors franchisee since 2001
Part of a select Pillar To Post Home Inspectors franchisee group called
Navigators which meets regularly to discuss business issues,
revenue growth, and accountability

I totally get it. You hate meetings. You think a "good meeting" is an oxymoron. You may have even opened your franchise because you wanted to make certain you never had to attend another dumb corporate meeting in your lifetime. If that sounds like you, here is my question: Did you think when you bought your franchise, it would only be about what *you* want? This might be true to a point, but when the reality that trying to do it all yourself takes a huge toll on your life, it's time to reconsider that premise.

Jeff Mackey explained in our interview that his decision to reinvest in his business included adding key personnel and moving his in-home office *out of the house*. We did not discuss how Jeff communicated his goals with his growing team, but based on his success, I know he did. I also know he held team members accountable. This chapter shows you one way to do it that worked like clockwork for my growing business quarter by quarter, year by year, for well over a decade. It will work for you.

Start by reframing your thinking. When you decided to hire the best possible staff your business could afford, you gained a team of people who *want more*. They want goals, feedback, and more information. They want to be recognized publicly, in front of their co-workers. They want to know the plan, as well as who is supposed to do what and when. Unless you like constant one-on-one meetings and aren't into team-building, your world needs a systematic communication forum for sitting down with those people you're counting on who are counting on you. Meetings are the best way to keep your business on track with accountability firmly intact.

Your challenge? Making your meetings productive, engaging, and results-oriented so accountability is a built-in value of your culture that starts with you. *You* set the tone for efficiency and consideration of personal and professional schedules by making a plan in advance for the year. Yes, you really *can* do this, and yes, you probably really *should* to do this if you want to make the changes that get you where you want to go this year.

Meetings and accountability are in the Method Management Pillar because they are a vital part of the success framework. I'll explain why and how meetings will make your life and your business better and easier, and how an Annual Meeting Plan allows you to build in accountability.

Why Have an Annual Meeting Plan?

An Annual Meeting Plan is an incredibly valuable tool because pre-set dates and agendas are laid out in advance with clear expectations for attendance and preparation. The agendas include reporting results, discussing problems, identifying opportunities, and fine-tuning the operation for the coming months. This pre-set communication forum helps you start to gain control over your business *and* your life. Especially once you've mastered and fine-tuned it. I'll show you one way to do it, and then you can design your own Annual Meeting Plan (AMP). And no, your attendance is not always required.

As many of you know, especially multi-unit owners, when your business grows so do the complexities and complications, especially if you aren't prepared. Luckily, I figured this out right before my local market got extremely competitive and our first expansion was almost complete. My primary goal was to cut back on unnecessary communication. It did that and much, much more.

The Case for Meetings as a Solid Investment of Time

When you implement an AMP, your employees will appreciate and respect you for creating a calmer, more secure environment where expectations are clear and accountability is in full view. Picture a workplace where stress is lowered across the board, excitement is building, and your sanity is squarely intact because you are in control of your business, not the other way around. Here are some of the benefits of well-planned meetings:

- **Planned meetings are opportunities to build teams, careers, and revenue.** The better your team, the better your revenue—and building careers equates to building deep loyalty. Higher-quality decision-making happens as teams mature, leading to increased loyalty and more people focused on the business.

- **Planned meetings provide regular opportunities to capture valuable ideas.** No more hallway interruptions to share an idea, stops by your office to run something by you, or random phone, text, or email interruptions. Like me, you probably want to hear about new ideas or recurring problems, just not at that moment. Instead of discouraging motivated employees by putting them off or not giving them our focused attention, planned meetings provide more time for givers to think through their ideas and allow you to give these employees your full attention.

- **Planned meetings offer a venue for solving problems properly, at the right time, with the right input.** Many issues warrant thought and discussion in a team setting with the right people present and focused. Addressing problems was a standing agenda item at our monthly and quarterly manager meetings. The protocol was that if a problem wasn't resolved before the next meeting, it was up to the initiator to put it on the agenda and lead the discussion. *Bam.*

Benefits of Having an Annual Meeting Plan

I'm going to share with you the full Annual Meeting Plan I implemented at my childcare franchise and break down the components and purposes of the quarterly, monthly, and weekly operations meetings. But first, in case you are feeling skeptical (and I understand that), I want you to hear what my former General Manager Tracy Musgrave, now elementary school program director at Central Florida YMCA in Orlando, says about planning meetings this way. Once we adopted this method for planning our meetings and adapted to it, we never looked back. Here's Tracy:

"It's hard to get invested in something when there is not a clear plan for the success of the business. When we sat down and made and agreed on our plan, it was like we had a roadmap for the year. We knew what was expected each month and how we were going to get there. Our meetings kept everyone checked in, on track, and able to see what needed to be changed."

Tracy was emphatic when she told me reviewing the business plan in the beginning of the year and building the programs as a team made her feel like she owned a piece of the business, and that made the team invested in the success. I think she would add, if you asked her, that the success, and the bonus checks that followed, felt pretty darn good. She is working hard to implement a similar meeting plan in her current role.

Here are some of the benefits of setting up an Annual Meeting Plan:

- **An Annual Meeting Plan eliminates the frustration of having to find a time and date that works for your staff, your managers, and your business.** I silently applaud when I see businesses post signs like "We will close from 2 to 4 p.m. on the third Thursday of the month for staff training." Easier said than done for many franchise owners. I found that having the schedule set in advance for the entire year is highly efficient and eliminates undue stress. It also eliminates excuses. Even emergencies dissipate when the expectation is that employees have a Plan B for most of the excuses we hear.

- **Annual Meeting Plan meetings are more effective and productive.** No surprise there. Agendas should be accessible to all key personnel and amended and refined as the date approaches. With agendas known in advance, last-minute preparations are noticeable, minimized, and seldom disruptive. You are responsible for the final version and for ensuring the quality, quantity, and flow are appropriate for the time allotted. Advance planning ensures that the people at the table are well-prepared, keeping discussions on track and lively. With pre-planned agendas, there are rarely surprises. You have time built in for a laugh, a shared story, consensus-building when an important idea or topic needs more time for further vetting.
- **A set format forces your management team (and you) to be accountable.** And I mean accountable not only to the meeting process itself, but also to your annual plans for programs and revenue goals. The right people are assembled, at the right time, and accountability is intact.

Constructing an Annual Meeting Plan

1. **Annual Managers Meeting**

   In early January, this all-day Saturday meeting was held at my home or other off-site location and communicated in writing two to three weeks in advance. I prepared lunch in advance or had it catered, with plenty of snacks and beverages as well. I usually had a kick-off gift of some kind such as a new folio with their initials or a fancy planner. I went out of my way to be a good hostess for my honored guests, and lunchtime was designated as a time for catching up and sharing stories, no business!

Purpose: "Sell" the new revenue numbers and the annual programs that are going to drive the revenue to the management team. Their buy-in was critical before implementing any plan for a successful year. The meeting preparation was on me. I set the quarterly targets and the management bonus plan in advance and had the prior years' data and trends formatted for easy review. This meeting also included the first-quarter (Q1) Manager Meeting and first month (M1) Manager Meeting.

The managers left this meeting with a concrete plan and renewed motivation for the coming year. The team-building that is derived from spending a full day together is an important component for gaining agreement and commitment for the annual plan. I viewed it as my bonus for a well-thought-out agenda, proper preparation, and hosting the event in my home or other off-site location. If you are just starting out, it may be just you and two employees or one manager and an up-and-comer on your team. You are never too small to hold this meeting. Team building is career building and a great investment of resources.

When you share a cohesive, well-thought-out plan with specific programming goals and plenty of time to implement and execute, reach around and pat yourself on the back. You have just added a layer, using Method Management with the Loyalty Pillar and the Strategic Leadership Pillar while your primary focus was the Money Metrics Pillar. That's a 4 Pillars Approach synergy homerun. And there is more to come.

2. **Quarterly (Q1 – Q4) Managers Meeting**

You hold three of these per year (Q1 is included in the Annual Manager Meeting). I planned and led this meeting, which was for managers only.

Purpose: Evaluate the quarterly revenue results and determine whether we had met our goals and could award bonus money. We looked at the individual specific program goals and discussed what was working well and what needed enhancing or changing before discussing the revenue goal for the coming quarter. I broke it down by month with specific targets and suggestions for capturing more revenue. We moved then to operations, staffing, and events, including the upcoming Quarterly Staff Meeting. We adjourned the meeting stress-free, with a quarterly calendar in place, energized and confident that our planning was thorough and the responsibilities for executing were in place for the next three months.

The quarterly meeting agendas and dates were kept on the company server for all managers to see and comment. Everyone had a part, and I vetted ideas for inclusion before making changes or adding to the agenda. The outline was consistent from Q1 to Q4, and everyone knew their role. The meeting was scheduled at the very end of the quarter from 10 a.m. to 2 p.m. and lunch was brought in. A supervisor-level staff member handled the front office so we could meet without interruption. Plan a time that can work well for your business and your manager(s). The first monthly meeting of the quarter was always included in our Quarterly Planning Meeting, eliminating the need for four monthly meetings.

3. **Quarterly (Q1 – Q4) Staff Meeting**

Held three or four times a year, this was planned by my managers and me. I opened and closed the meeting, and managers each took a part of the agenda. In lieu of the fourth-quarter meeting, we often had a fall or holiday staff event.

Purpose: One part team-building, one part social, and one part business. Know that going in and you won't be disappointed *or disappoint.* Depending on the size of your business and your hours of operation, this meeting can be very tricky (and costly) to pull off. However, pull off you must, twice a year at a minimum. Four times a year is better.

We tried to keep them fun and always focused on recognizing employees and the differences they made individually and collectively. I scheduled (and paid them) 1.5 hours each for the time. We tried to start on time (not easy) and always ended on time. If we could work in a career development exercise or personal assessment (like a free Emotional Intelligence online survey) then we were doing really well.

Don't make this meeting too serious unless you have problems in your business that you need to address. Your staff loves to see you, and this is one more way to build layers of loyalty and practice good leadership.

4. **Monthly (M1 – M12) Managers Meeting**

   Held nine times per year, this was planned and led by the managers and focused on the upcoming month. I usually dropped in for a portion of the meeting in case they wanted to run something past me, but I was clear that this was their meeting.

   The Monthly Manager Meetings were held at the end of the month, usually a Thursday, and lasted two to three hours. No special accommodations were made for coverage. The agenda was always on the company server and managers could add to it throughout the month without approval or prior review by me. The final weekly meeting of the month was incorporated into the monthly meeting.

   Purpose: Review the revenue, make sure final plans for the next month were in place, and discuss any "red flags" and "white flags." This was our trigger for discussing current difficult clients (children or parents), staff, or other urgent matters that needed vetting. Red was for alerting purposes and white was for resolution or closure. Outcomes and lessons learned were discussed at the next monthly meeting, or sooner if needed. New processes and procedures sometimes grew from these important discussions. Consider developing a code word and defining your organization's red and white flags.

5. **Weekly Managers Operations Meeting**

   The weekly Managers Operations Meeting was usually less than an hour long and was held on Thursday afternoon or during lunch on Friday. It was included in the Monthly Managers Meeting, eliminating the need for a separate operations discussion.

   Purpose: Finalize the staff schedule, review new weekly rosters, and discuss any other details that needed to be covered to ensure a successful upcoming week *with no surprises*. At the end of the meeting, the late payment report was reviewed so parents could be reminded they had not paid tuition for the week or notified of an impending disenrollment. I did not attend this meeting but often offered to buy lunch for attendees. Final weekly reports were put into my inbox by Friday afternoon.

On the following page is a sample Annual Meeting Plan and the one I adapted for my franchise. As you go through it, think of how you could change it to fit your business. As we discussed in Planning Your Profits, if you are ready to put the 4 Pillars Approach to work for your franchise, I recommend an owner's private Annual Planning Meeting in late November or early December to review the current year-end revenue and budget numbers and set the revenue and program goals for the coming year. I recommend reviewing and distributing your Annual Meeting Plan when you have your Annual Managers Meeting in early January.

Sample Annual Meeting Plan

Q1 – January	First Saturday 5-6 hours off-site	**January is key to focus and motivate your entire staff** Annual Managers Meeting – Set Program & Revenue Goals (Included 1st Quarter & 1st Monthly Meetings) **Q1** Managers Meeting (MM) + Month 1 (M1) MM
	Mid-Month	Q1 Staff Meeting (SM) – 60-90 minutes
	Weekly	Managers Operations Meeting (MOM) – 1 hour
	Last Week	M2 + MOM – 2-3 hours
February – M2	Weekly	MOM
	Month-End	M3 MM + MOM
March – M3	Weekly	MOM
	Month-End	**Q2** MM + M4 MM + MOM – 3-4 hours
Q2 – April		**Review & Refresh Programs, Energize – Make It Fun**
	Mid-Month	Q2 SM
	Weekly	MOM
	Last Week	M5 MM + MOM
May – M5	Weekly	MOM
	Last Week	M6 MM + MOM
	Mid-Month	Pre-Camp Bus Driver Team Meeting – Owner-Led
June – M6	Weekly	MOM
	Last Week	**Q3** MM + M7 MM + MOM – 3-4 hours
Q3 – July		**Don't Lose Focus Mid-Year: Stay Engaged!**
	Mid-Month	Q3 SM
	Weekly	MOM
	Last Week	M8 MM + MOM
August – M8	Weekly	MOM
	Last Week	M9 MM + MOM
September – M9	Weekly	MOM
	Last Week	**Q4** MM + M10 MM + MOM – 3-4 hours
Q4 – October		**Final Push to Make the Number – Be Coach & Cheerleader**
	Mid-Month	Q4 SM or Holiday Event in December
	Weekly	MOM
	Last Week	M11 MM + MOM
November – M11	Weekly	MOM
	Last Week	M12 MM + MOM
	Last Week	Owner's Annual Planning Meeting for New Year **Clear Your Calendar – It's Time to Plan for Next Year**
December – M12	Weekly	MOM
	Mid-Month	**Announce Date, Time & Place of Annual Mgrs. Meeting**
	Last Week	MOM – Gratitude Time

Annual Meeting Plan – Immediate Benefits to Your Business

Here are some benefits to incorporating an Annual Meeting Plan. Some of these are from my experience, and others are great ideas I found in a textbook I use titled *The Management of Strategy in the Marketplace*, from "Chapter 2: Group Dynamics, Processes and Teamwork" by Joyce E.A. Russell, University of Maryland, and Jacquelyn DeMatteo Jacobs, University of Tennessee.

1. Goals are set, agreed upon, and communicated—for the year.
2. Results are regularly reviewed and reported, reinforcing accountability.
3. Interruptions are minimized because managers know the right time to discuss and clarify.
4. Efficiencies occur because there is a method for consistent communication of ideas, problems, and results.
5. Stress is minimized because expectations are clear.
6. Efficiency and productivity increase because there is a time for all important business communications.
7. Managers are more creative and innovative because they have time to meaningfully converse with staff and clients, which allows them to gain insights and fresh ideas.
8. Franchisees gain "white space" time for creative and innovative thinking, thereby helping ensure future sustainable revenue growth.
9. You are developing your managers and others in ways that few others would. They learn and grow through the annual meeting process and the trust that you bestow on them. This benefits you, your business, and their careers. It helps pave the way for your possible future expansion.
10. You gain respect from managers and others when they understand and experience the calm and secure environment your planning has created.

Informal Communication

Certainly not everything should be addressed in a meeting. Informal and interpersonal communication is paramount for a healthy and happy work environment and a key to good leadership. This model allows your managers and you the time and space to build stronger relationships throughout the organization and successfully guide your business throughout the year. Interactions become more heartfelt and genuine when stress is decreased and the environment is safe. Conflicts are more easily identified and resolved, and gossip is greatly decreased, all because of your planning.

Creating a secure culture with clear boundaries, accountability, and set channels for running the business successfully is good for everyone. It starts with you setting the expectations based on your goals and plan for the year and having the discipline to hold yourself accountable for the success of the business.

And *that is* sexy.

CHAPTER 17

Thrive through the Peaks *and* Valleys

You have to free yourself and your mind. Take your head "out of the basket" but keep an eye on the day-to-day operations in order to look for other opportunities. Otherwise, you will never grow.

Jehad "Jack" Hannoush

Lake Mary, Florida
Edible Arrangements Fruit Baskets and Bouquets franchisee since 2006
Multi-unit franchisee in Orlando/Central Florida

n the introduction, I discussed how in the early years of franchise ownership, I was significantly influenced by Dr. Spencer Johnson, noted author of *Who Moved My Cheese?* His book, *Peaks and Valleys: Making Good and Bad Times Work for You—at Work and in Life*, introduced a concept that stuck with me so much that I visualized it often.

The concept I'm referring to again is based on the theory that every business which remains open for even just a few years will experience peaks and valleys. When your business is at the top of a very high peak, it will eventually come down the other side to an equally deep valley. The peaks can make you think "I've got this!" when you don't and the valleys can be treacherous if you don't have a clear path out or plan well enough ahead. Even for seasoned franchisees.

An example would be the small business owners in the Sunbelt states of Florida, Texas, and Nevada. Because of the huge influx of new residents into these high-growth states, franchisees of all types thrived, including Kids 'R' Kids Academy, which had more locations in Texas than in many other states combined. Many had far to fall when the housing bubble burst in the Great Recession of 2008. I heard firsthand from some of our very best owners at our annual conference the fear that kind of uncertainty brings.

A similar but smaller bust happened in 2016 in North Dakota and parts of Texas when oil prices plummeted. Franchisees serving those communities were left reeling when the fracking and drilling slowed. Ironically, but not surprisingly, franchises that have a relatively high gasoline expense were enjoying additional profits from decreased expenses from this same cycle. A valley for some is a peak for others.

When I experienced similar peaks and valleys early in my business, you may recall that it was Dr. Johnson's book that motivated me to learn how to strengthen, protect, and grow my business the very best way I could. And as a leader, you should be committed to the same. Being firmly entrenched in reality is the best place to start.

Macro Forces 2.0

One of the realities of owning a business today is that there are so many macro and political forces that can seriously impact your business with little and sometimes zero warning. We touched briefly on this substantial list in the beginning of the book, but now we take a deeper dive in order to gain a complete understanding of why the 4 Pillars Approach works.

Besides normal economic cycles that occur every three to seven years, bubbles burst (dot-com, housing, energy) with widespread effects. There are acts of God, such as Superstorm Sandy of 2012, and decimating tornadoes impacting entire communities often full of franchised business owners. Acts of domestic and international terrorism, sadly, now occur on a regular basis, impacting the resort and travel industry like one-two punches in a round of boxing. As a nation, we have witnessed horrendous evil and hatred. Even peaceful equality demonstrations can close downtown streets, leaving franchises that sell sandwiches, personal services, or printing upside down for days. But that's not all.

Add to this list far-reaching changes in legislation such as healthcare reform, tax reform, Department of Labor rules that adjust the minimum wage rate, and our continuing battle to keep franchisees from being dumped and lumped into the larger, more restrictive and expensive employer category. These are examples of political and employment law changes that even with advance notice can suck your profit margin right off the page. Specific segments have their own unique challenges with state laws impacting certifications and certain kinds of licensing and inspection requirements.

I'm not trying to be a fear monger, just a realist. Being a good business owner cannot prevent macro forces from occurring, but you can lessen the severity of the impact on your business. When you strengthen, protect, and grow your business with the 4 Pillars Approach, you smooth out the landscape and create your own terrain.

Smooth Out the Landscape

My biggest takeaway from reading Johnson's book was that it's best to avoid the thrill ride by managing your business in ways that smooth out the landscape. I decided right then that I'd take serene rolling hills over peaks and valleys when it came to my business. Armed with self-knowledge about my personal needs and limitations, including a *touch* of attention-deficit disorder, and my ambition, I had already built in some boundaries for the amount of stress and drama I'd allow into my life. That is, after all, one of the biggest reasons you and I decided to purchase a franchised business, isn't it? We want to gain control of our life and our future.

By working the 4 Pillars Approach tools and practices into your organization, there is no need to fear for the worst and hope for the best when the next big fat bubble bursts or the Federal Reserve raises interest rates twice in one year. While the 4 Pillars can't prevent a hurricane from closing down your restaurant for a few days or stop a crazed person from inflicting horrendous violence in a downtown nightclub or church adjacent to your sandwich or printing franchise, it can position you in such a way that you will come out nearly unscathed. You may even be a hero when you're done because, as a 4 Pillars franchise owner and all-around good person, you will show your leadership and express how much you care about your employees, your clients, and all those people in your community who are also impacted. Because you *do* care.

With the 4 Pillars Approach to smooth out the landscape, my franchise functioned at a consistently high level with annual revenue increases straight through numerous macro events including the Great Recession until I sold in 2012. It's that powerful. The final expansion in 2010 had no hiccups and left me with no regrets. That's why I'm so earnest in my belief that this approach can strengthen, protect, and grow your business even when the next tough cycle comes around. And rest assured, it will come. I want you to be ready.

Be Effectual and Create Your Own Terrain

I'm very honored to now teach as a professor at Rollins College in my hometown of Winter Park, Florida. Over the past two years, I've learned much from many of my colleagues and was glad to be introduced to a textbook titled *Effectual Entrepreneurship* by Stuart Read, Saras Sarasvathy, Nick Dew, and Robert Wiltbank.

Effectuation has become popular term in college and university business departments that teach entrepreneurship and is a theory that is used to explain how successful entrepreneurs think about their businesses. Effectual entrepreneurs take advantage of the unexpected by embracing surprise, exert control by influencing their environment, and create opportunities to transform and grow their business. To me, that explained if not the entire ownership journey, at least a huge chunk of the past 15 years. I confess, I was surprised that what entrepreneurs do can even be taught.

It took me a few months to completely absorb this theory and I was skeptical for months. However, the more I read, absorbed, and discussed examples in the classroom, I realized it was "effectuation" principles applied to my franchised business that helped me *create* and *transform* the environment into a healthy, thriving terrain, rather than accept the less effectual peaks and valleys thrill ride. That smooth terrain helped me avoid and manage risks inherent in climbing up one side and sliding down the other. It helped me stay focused on the business at all times. However, it wasn't until I was in my second year of teaching and about halfway into the writing process that I realized how effectuation principles and actions could bolster the bottom line of almost any franchised business. That's when I met Kevin and Jami Wray, a husband and wife ownership team of a Peterbrooke Chocolatier franchise down the street from Rollins College.

As a frequent patron of their delicious fairly-traded chocolate, I knew it was a well-run business. I invited Kevin to be a guest speaker and, through his presentation, learned how he and Jami bought their franchise when it was in the red and turned it into a top performer in the Peterbrooke system. That's when I had the true "ah-ha" moment; that the 4 Pillars Approach is in many ways, based on effectuation principles. At that instant, I understood, on a much deeper level, why my business thrived at times when others struggled and was compelled to bring this instructional information to you.

That's also when I decided that I needed to interview other top performing franchisees. I wanted to show, to prove really, how the 4 Pillars Approach will take you exactly where you want to go, regardless of segment or brand. That is, as long as you don't pull back.

You Might Be Tempted, but Don't Be

It's human nature, when you own a franchise or any business, to be tempted to pull back on your engagement when the cash is flowing, the employees are happy, and your clients are referring their friends and co-workers to you. What you now know is that if you do pull back, even a little, the layers will be missed and the pillars will not be balanced. And that makes your business vulnerable. In effect, by enjoying the view too long, you are choosing to create a peak that will result in a valley in mirror image.

Top-performing franchisees know it takes tremendous discipline to stay focused and maintain full engagement and accountability when times are great. They say "No thank you" to the roller coaster ride, preferring to create a smooth terrain that leads to greater enjoyment of their business. The vast majority, the 80 to 90 percent of franchisees and small business owners, are tempted. *Don't be tempted.*

Characteristics of Franchisees that Leverage the 4 Pillars Approach

- They **Build Layers of Loyalty**, sharing their success with those who helped create it by celebrating milestones, marking anniversaries, and acknowledging loyal employees and clients in meaningful ways. They know which clients, employees, and community partners are their Sweet Spots and have designed programs that ensure their loyalty while actively seeking more.

- They **Lead Strategically** by actively looking for new opportunities to grow their business. They embrace surprise when the unexpected happens, turning it into ways to strengthen, protect, and grow their business.

- They **Develop Money Metrics** and are laser-focused on intimately knowing their revenue, expense, and profit numbers and how changes in any of these impacts the others.

- They are **Method Managers** who share their systematic and methodical best practices with other franchisees, support franchisor programs, and communicate innovative ideas for growing revenue and improving productivity and efficiency.

- They are among the **Top Tier** of their franchise system because they are on top of their businesses. Depending on their personal goals and timing, they readily explore options for expansion by buying a second (or fourth!) franchise because they have cash in the bank, passion for the brand, and the energy and joy to do it.

I want you to be one of these franchisees. I want you to have the same strength and resilience built into your business that these franchisees do. Let's look at several not-so-uncommon scenarios that might make you feel you have no control over as a business owner and apply the 4 Pillars to gain control.

3 Scenarios That Can Cause a Valley but Won't

Don't dismiss any of these examples as out of the realm. If you have not yet encountered these or something similar, you probably will. Your task will be to adapt these to your franchise and be prepared if and when they should happen.

1) Acts of God

Acts of God create deep valleys unless you are prepared. Prepared means having enough insurance and enough cash flow to sustain at least two weeks of no income. In 2004, Orlando had the toughest hurricane season on record with three back-to-back brutal storms in six weeks, extolling hardship and widespread damage. It was a very difficult period emotionally and financially for everyone, including all small businesses.

Ironically, as I wrote this final chapter, Hurricane Matthew of 2016 passed through Florida as the first major storm since then. That caused me to reflect on what it took to get through those three hurricanes in 2004 and how much it tested my leadership. I also thought of the many area franchisees who had to shut down during the government curfew imposed during the storm and wondered how or if they had a plan to communicate with their clients and employees. The answer, I knew, was probably not. Thankfully, it was just a two-day closure for most, but it easily could have been a week.

The 4 Pillars Approach will strengthen, protect, and yes, even grow your business during Acts of God *because you demonstrate:*

- **Strategic Leadership** – Set up a communication protocol if you have not already. You should have supplies on hand to prepare your facility. Communicate directly and often with your staff. Many also have families, so find out who can be flexible if you need to open or close in a rush. Make courtesy calls to your clients who may have appointments in order to reschedule.
- **Employee Loyalty** – This is when you demonstrate fairness and caring toward your staff and their families. They'll remember. Consider giving your scheduled staff the same pay (I called it a Hurricane Day) as if they had worked. This is not the time to be ungrateful or miserly.

- **Client Loyalty** – With the back-to-back hurricanes, I pro-rated tuition and credited extra vacation weeks for those who chose to stay off work each week. Many of my clients had reduced paychecks. We got through this together.
- **Community Loyalty** – Bring sandwiches or whatever you can to first responders and others who may not have fared as well. Think of some way to give back to show yours is a business that cares.
- **Solid Metrics** – You project calm strength during a crisis because you have the cash flow to see you through two tough weeks and a line of credit established in advance for emergencies such as this.

2) Economic Downturns

There are many reasons businesses experience downturns. Some will be more severe than others, depending on your location and the impetus of the downturn. Some will come with warning and others will not. The 4 Pillars Approach will get you through economic downturns *because you:*

- **Know Your Numbers** – You will know where you can adjust quickly without impacting quality. Do this very early in the down cycle and keep a close eye on the weekly reports.
- **Plan Your Profits** – That plan includes increased revenue. Your programs are well-thought-out, in place, and layered for greater impact and synergies. This is not the time to pull back.
- **Connect with Your Community** – You enlist strong **partners** and establish solid **community** relationships that will continue to refer business because you have consistently demonstrated you are in business for the right reasons, which include supporting them and being supported by them.
- **You Are an Engaged Owner** – You ask questions and anticipate problems at scheduled Manager Meetings, so it will not be disconcerting to others when you ask for more specific information in order to hunker down with your managers to plan and prepare for potential cutbacks.

3) Changing Markets

Changes in your local and regional market can create financial stress in your business and a deep valley if you aren't using the 4 Pillars Approach. Valleys can be caused by new competitors opening, a large employer relocating or shutting down, and low unemployment numbers, making it difficult to attract and keep good employees.

The 4 Pillars Approach ensures your growth plans remain on track because *you have*:

- A **True Competitive Advantage** and **Client Loyalty Layers** – These strategies ensure your clients will stay your clients so you don't look (or feel!) desperate and beg them to stay.
- **Efficiency and Revenue-Building Programs** – These include staff incentives for achieving performance goals and Incorporating new ways to improve your operation and expand your client base.
- **Pre-Planned Quarterly Meetings** – Your meetings prevent stress and insecurity in the workplace because your agenda always includes a brainstorming session—and this one will focus on new ways to find and keep good employees. Maybe it's time to have an open house or job fair?
- **Career Development** – Plans for yourself and your staff can pay big dividends when your market changes because their maturity and loyalty will make a difference to your business.

This Is Your Future

It is my sincere desire that you take the information I have shared throughout this book to heart and put it to good use in order to achieve the goals and success you want and deserve. I further hope you were willing to take stock of your current business situation, including an honest assessment of your business and leadership strengths, weaknesses, fears, motivation, and outlook for the future. And finally, I hope you made a decision to build the 4 Pillars Approach into your franchise.

If you did, this is a snapshot of your future—and if you didn't, it's never too late to start. Never.

You feel confident and engaged. You enjoy the day-to-day rewards and challenges your business brings because your franchise revenue is growing and the challenges are not as stressful as they used to be. You have time to ask your employees if they enjoyed their weekend and express your concern when they are going through rough times. Your clients know who you are because you are present in your business and you now have time to exchange pleasantries and ask for valuable feedback. You have community partners who call you when there is a meaningful opportunity to give back because they know you truly care about the community. They frequently send you high-quality employees, personally use your services, and refer new clients.

You are noticeably more relaxed at home, have more time for your passions outside of work and take care of yourself because you know how much money you are going to make this year and have programs in place to get you there. Your family and friends ask what has changed because you're not constantly on your phone or checking your messages. You know it's due to managers who are accountable and know exactly how much revenue they need to bring in this month in order for the business to be successful this year. Competitors are not a threat to your business, and if a new one comes, so be it. You now have time built into your week to work "on your business, not in your business" and that newfound "white space" includes a competitive survey and some fresh ideas you've been processing. You'll be able to adjust, add, and pivot so they "keep coming back."

As a franchise owner who has built the 4 Pillars layer by layer to strengthen, protect, and grow your business, you no longer lie awake at night wondering whether you did the right thing when you bought your franchise or added a second one last year. You know you did.

You feel in control of your business because *you are*. You are making the money you want, need, and deserve to earn without worrying about the future because you are highly focused on your success this year and know that next year's planning will again be guided by the 4 Pillars Approach.

You worked hard to get here and enjoy every moment – as it should be.

Most people wouldn't even have dared to try. But you did. And it was worth it. You are proud of your hard-earned, well-deserved success because you built something that is meaningful to you, your staff, your clients, your family, and your community.

You sit back and truly enjoy your business and your life. Congratulations. *You've got this.*

FRANCHISOR DESCRIPTIONS AND CONTACT INFORMATION

The franchisors and franchisees who assisted with this project did so without hesitation, and I am deeply grateful for their support. My goal for choosing which companies and brands to interview was to try and reflect, as closely as possible, the general segmentation of our industry. While I did not have succeeded entirely, I did my resolute best, and believe I came fairly close. No commitments were requested or made nor monies exchanged throughout the process for this assistance.

To the franchise representatives: I'm extremely grateful to you for going above and beyond. Your willingness to introduce me to your top-performing franchisees and other key personnel within your organizations is a testament to your passion for your brand, for the industry, and for the success of others.

To the franchisees and company executives I interviewed: Thank you for your transparency, generosity of your time, and your commitment to making your business the best it can be. You continue to inspire me and will, no doubt, inspire many others.

Chapter 1 – Kids 'R' Kids Learning Academies

Kids 'R' Kids Learning Academies is a privately owned preschool franchising system that educates and cares for children from six weeks through 12 years. All Learning Academies are individually owned and operated. Each owner is coached from the very beginning through the corporate headquarters to employ skilled teachers and staff to provide quality care and early childhood education using the company's exclusive curriculum. The company's philosophy is to "Hug First, Then Teach." The founders, Pat and Janice Vinson, are still active in the company, which they refer to as "an overnight success that has been in the making since 1988."

kidsrkidsfranchise.com

800-279-0033

Chapter 1 – BrightStar Care

BrightStar Care is the franchise leader in the fast-growing home care industry. BrightStar Care is a unique international brand offering a full range of companion care, personal care, skilled nursing, and staffing services. The average revenue for BrightStar Care locations was $1.6 million as reported in the 2017 BrightStar Care Franchise Disclosure Document (FDD).

BrightStarCare.com

877-689-6898

Chapter 2 – Wild Birds Unlimited

Our franchisees say that interacting with customers is one of the most rewarding aspects of owning a Wild Birds Unlimited store. You make a difference in your customers' lives by helping them connect with birds and nature. You also serve the community by providing the best local advice on how to enjoy the hobby, which differentiates you from big-box stores and other competitors.

wbu.com

wbufranchise.com

888-730-7108, Ext. 119

Chapter 3 – Dream Vacations

Dream Vacations is part of World Travel Holdings, the world's largest cruise agency and award-winning leisure travel company. As an experiential brand, Dream Vacations is the only travel franchise opportunity to have a name that speaks to the variety of vacation experiences its franchisees sell. With unrivaled buying power, franchisees can provide competitive prices and exclusive offers when selling memorable vacation experiences such as cruises, resort stays, and land tours.

DreamVacationsFranchise.com

facebook.com/DreamVacationsFranchise

@Dream_Franchise on Twitter

Chapter 4 – Sonny's BBQ

Sonny's BBQ is a franchised barbecue restaurant chain founded by Floyd "Sonny" Tillman in Gainesville, Florida, in 1968, and is known for its Southern hospitality. Sonny's BBQ specializes in Southern-style BBQ and has 113 restaurants across eight Southeastern states.

sonnysbbq.com

407-660-8888

Chapter 5 – Freddy's Frozen Custard

Freddy's Frozen Custard and Steakburgers is a fast-casual restaurant franchise that brings to life the America of the late 1940s and early 1950s, a post-war era of pride and values focusing on unity and quality family time. Menu items are cooked to order and include lean ground beef steakburgers, Vienna beef hot dogs, and creamy frozen custard treats. Franchise sites are modeled after the original Freddy's location opened in Wichita, Kansas, in 2002. Captioned photos in the restaurants are genuine photos of co-founder Freddy and feature his life growing up on a farm, his service in the U.S. Army, and time as a family and business man. The business model revolves around genuine guest hospitality and service with a smile.

freddysusa.com/franchising/

Chapter 6 – uBreakiFix

Founded in 2009, uBreakiFix specializes in the repair of small electronics, ranging from smartphones, game consoles, tablets, computers and everything in between. Cracked screens, water damage, software issues, camera issues, and most any other problem can be repaired by visiting uBreakiFix stores across the

U.S. and in Canada. uBreakiFix is the official walk-in repair partner for Pixel, a phone by Google.

ubreakifix.com

franchising@ubreakifix.com

Chapter 7 – Firehouse Subs

Firehouse Subs is a fast casual restaurant chain with a passion for Hearty and Flavorful food, Heartfelt service, and Public Safety. Founded by former firefighting brothers Robin and Chris Sorensen in 1994, Firehouse Subs is a brand built on decades of fire and police service, hot subs, steamed and piled higher with the highest-quality meats and cheeses and its commitment to saving lives through the establishment of the non-profit Firehouse Subs Public Safety Foundation which has donated more than $29 million to hometown heroes. There are more than 1,100 Firehouse Subs in 44 states, Puerto Rico, Canada and Mexico, and is recognized as one of the best franchises in the country.

firehousesubs.com

franchising@firehousesubs.com

877-887-8330

Chapter 8 – Anytime Fitness

Ranked #1 Top Global franchise by *Entrepreneur*, Anytime Fitness is the world's largest and fastest-growing co-ed fitness club franchise with more than 3,000 clubs in 50 states and 20 countries. Clubs are open 24 hours a day, and the model works well in large and small communities. Previous fitness industry experience is not needed to be a successful franchisee. All you need is the passion to help people and to follow the business model.

anytimefitness.com

info@anytimefitness.com

800-704-5004

Chapter 9 – Impact Properties

Impact Properties owns and operates more than 50 franchised units across national hotel, restaurant, and retail brands including CARSTAR and RAC

(Rent-A-Center) throughout the Southeastern U.S, and is headquartered in Tampa, Florida. Impact Properties was referred to the author by BurgerFi corporate headquarters.

impact-properties.com

(813) 287-0907

Chapter 9 – BurgerFi

Established in 2011, BurgerFi is among the nation's fastest-growing better burger concepts with 100 restaurants open and operating. Founded by gourmet chefs committed to serving fresh food of transparent quality, BurgerFi uses only 100 percent natural Angus beef patties that are free from antibiotics, steroids, and growth hormones. The BurgerFi franchise system has been developed to create consistency in design, operations, and the overall customer experience. The franchise is ranked #4 on Fast Casual's 2017 Top 100 Movers & Shakers list; and one of the top 10 fastest- and smartest-growing brands in franchising and a leader in the better burger category by *Franchise Times* in its Fast and Serious list for 2017.

burgerfi.com

gbuckley@burgerfi.com

888-799-5528

Chapter 10 – European Wax Center

European Wax Center (EWC) brings a unique waxing expertise and beauty experience to women throughout the USA. The setting: a modern environment with crisp, clean lines, private waxing suites, providing the most professionally trained waxing experts, with exceptional service, along with proprietary products to use at home as well as in center. EWC enables everyone to reveal beautiful skin and feel unapologetically confident. As a result, today, EWC is recognized as one of the fastest-growing companies in the beauty lifestyle category.

waxcenter.com

franchise.waxcenter.com

Chapter 11 – Style Encore

Style Encore buys and sells gently used apparel, shoes, handbags, and accessories for women. Rapidly growing with more than 58 franchised stores in the United States and Canada and 12 more opening soon, the retailer aims to be the preferred store for fashionistas, bargain hunters, and recycling-conscious women by focusing on the latest styles and hottest brands, all in great condition. Style Encore is franchised by Winmark Corporation, which also franchises Plato's Closet, Play It Again Sports, Once Upon a Child, and Music Go Round.

style-encore.com

winmarkfranchises.com/style-encore/

(866) 591-1757

Chapter 11 – Play It Again Sports

Play It Again Sports leads the nation in the buying and selling of quality used sports and fitness equipment. There are more than 280 franchised stores in the United States and Canada. Play It Again Sports buys, sells, and trades quality used and new brand name sports and fitness equipment. Play It Again Sports is franchised by Winmark Corporation, which also franchises Plato's Closet, Once Upon A Child, Music Go Round, and Style Encore.

playitagainsports.com

winmarkfranchises.com/play-it-again-sports/

(866) 591-1757

Chapter 12 – Great Clips

Great Clips is a 100 percent franchised company with more than 4,100 salons across North America—each one offering a great haircut at a great location at a great price. Great Clips prided itself on making it easy for customers to get a great haircut at a time and place that's convenient for them. That's why Great Clips salons are open evenings and weekends, no appointments necessary. Great Clips salon owners employ 40,000 stylists who receive ongoing training to learn advanced skills and the latest trends.

greatclips.com

800-473-2825

Chapter 13 – Maaco

MAACO is North America's body shop, franchised with over 500 owner operators whose centers boast system-wide sales approaching a billion dollars. The company celebrates extraordinary brand recognition and 45 years without any national competition. New franchisees receive three weeks of training at the corporate headquarters plus three weeks of on-the-job training for themselves and their employees. The unprecedented and continued operational support positions candidates from all walks of life, including those with no automotive experience, to thrive in the system.

maacofranchise.com

asuggs@maaco.com

800-275-5200

Chapter 14 – Golden Corral

With more than 40 years of success and nearly 500 locations, Golden Corral is recognized as America's #1 buffet and grill by *Nation's Restaurant News*. The concept is a proven winner—a high-value, family-oriented lunch and dinner buffet with breakfast every weekend. Golden Corral is the first-choice franchise brand for savvy restaurant operators looking to expand their local dining market share or successful franchisees seeking to diversify their portfolio with a proven high-revenue brand.

goldencorralfranchise.com

abagwell@goldencorral.net

800-284-5673

Chapter 14 – Brightway Insurance

Brightway Insurance is a property/casualty insurance agency selling through a network of franchised locations. Brightway provides its franchisees with a comprehensive system of support that lets them focus on selling; this approach lets franchisees outsell their competition 3:1. Brightway customers enjoy choice in insurance carriers, expert, in-person counsel, and a single 800 number to call to get all of their insurance needs met.

BrightwayDifference.com

Chapter 14 – Chick-fil-A

Chick-fil-A is a family owned and privately held restaurant company founded in 1967. Devoted to serving the local communities in which its franchised restaurants operate, and known for its original chicken sandwich, Chick-fil-A serves freshly prepared food in more than 2,200 locations in 46 states. Known for "providing value through service," and awarded "the most polite restaurant in the country" in 2016 in the *QSR* magazine Drive-Thru Performance Study, Chick-fil-A was the only restaurant brand named to the "Top 10 Best Companies to Work For" by 24/7 Wall Street.

chick-fil-a.com

Chapter 15 – Philly Pretzel Factory

Philly Pretzel Factory offers consumers fun and satisfying snacks and meal replacement items at a great value that are "served hot outta the oven." Philly Pretzel Factory was founded in 1998 by college buddies Dan DiZio and Len Lehman and has grown into the largest Philly-style pretzel bakery in the world, feeding customers at more than 170 franchised locations across the country. Philly Pretzel Factory franchises are located in stand-alone bakeries, in transportation and entertainment venues, and in the nation's largest retailer, Walmart.

phillypretzelfactory.com

ownappf.com

Chapter 16 – Pillar To Post Home Inspectors

With more than 550 locations in 49 states and eight Canadian provinces, Pillar To Post is the largest home inspection franchise company in North America and was the first to bring technology to the home inspection business with electronic inspection reports. The company has repeatedly been named No. 1 in the home inspection category (*Entrepreneur* 500, January 2016) and as a Top Service Franchise (*Franchise Business Review*, July 2016) and is a favorite among veterans looking for a career.

pillartopost.com

877-604-8584

Chapter 17 – Edible Arrangements

With more than 1,300 franchise locations, Edible Arrangements International LLC is the world's largest franchisor of shops offering creatively designed fresh-cut fruit arrangements. Since its founding in 1999, the company has been recognized as an industry leader, ranking first in its category in *Entrepreneur* magazine's annual "Franchise 500," *Entrepreneur's* Top 40 of "Fastest-Growing Franchises," and "America's Top Global Franchises" as well as being included among the *Inc.* 5000 list of the fastest-growing privately held companies. Edible Arrangements" fresh fruit arrangements, chocolate Dipped Fruit™, fresh fruit smoothies, and more can be enjoyed at franchise locations worldwide.

ediblearrangements.com

888-727-4258

ownafranchise@edible.com

BRING ADVENTURES IN FRANCHISE OWNERSHIP TO YOUR ORGANIZATION OR NEXT EVENT

Do you want franchise owners and general managers who are fully engaged, aligned with brand initiatives, and focused on increasing revenues—year after year? You might need a different kind of message … and a different kind of speaker.

In addition to teaching future entrepreneurs, Christy Wilson Delk is passionate about working directly with organizations as a speaker, workshop leader, and consultant for short-term engagements. The 4 Pillars Approach and the various aspects of *Adventures in Franchise Ownership* resonate with both large and small audiences who quickly recognize that Christy has, quite literally, been in their shoes. Her energy, humor, and down-to-earth approach ensure an engaging and memorable presentation from one who has truly "walked the talk."

CHRISTY'S COMMITMENT
AS YOUR SPEAKER OR WORKSHOP LEADER

- Franchisees will become intensely focused on their numbers and growth.
- Franchisees will have a tactical plan for intangibles like community engagement and building deep loyalty.
- Franchisees—new and seasoned—will be more motivated and invigorated.

CONNECT WITH CHRISTY

Let Christy know how the 4 Pillars Approach works in your business. Your story may be featured in one of her future articles, or you could even end up in her next book. Email Christy@ChristyWilsonDelk.com with your own adventures in franchising.

Christy offers periodic updates, constructive ideas, and best practices you may want to incorporate into your franchise. Visit www.ChristyWilsonDelk. com to learn more, read her bi-monthly articles, and connect via her social media channels.

LinkedIn: https://www.linkedin.com/in/ChristyWilsonDelk/
Twitter: https://twitter.com/WilsonDelk
Facebook: https://www.facebook.com/ChristyWilsonDelk
Instagram: https://www.instagram.com/ChristyWilsonDelk

ABOUT THE AUTHOR

After 17 years in corporate sales and distribution, Christy Wilson Delk decided to risk it all. In 1996, she sold her house and cashed out her 401(k) plan for the down payment on the $1.7 million-dollar Small Business Administration loan she needed to buy and build a Kids 'R' Kids Academy franchise in Orlando, Florida.

Over the next 15 years, Christy expanded twice and grew her business into one of the largest franchises in her industry before exiting successfully in 2012. Now, a full time professor at Rollins College and franchise industry contributing writer and speaker, Christy has turned her focus to helping others realize greater professional rewards through growing a successful business.

Christy has a B.A. in Psychology from the University of Florida and an MBA from Everest University. She is the proud mom of one son, and lives in a 100-year-old home in Winter Park, Florida, with an old hound dog and frisky cat.

Morgan James
Speakers Group

www.TheMorganJamesSpeakersGroup.com

We connect Morgan James published authors with live and online events and audiences who will benefit from their expertise.

Morgan James makes all of our titles available
through the Library for All Charity Organization.

www.LibraryForAll.org

Printed in the USA
CPSIA information can be obtained
at www.ICGtesting.com
JSHW021805040324
58562JS00004B/254